KNITTING
by
DESIGN

KNITTING

by

DESIGN

Gather Inspiration, Design Looks, and Knit 15 Fashionable Projects

Emma Robertson

PHOTOGRAPHS BY MAX WANGER

CHRONICLE BOOKS

SAN FRANCISCO

Library of Congress Cataloging-in-Publication Data:
Robertson, Emma.
  Knitting by design: gather inspiration, design looks,
  and knit 15 fashionable projects / Emma Robertson.
    pages cm
  ISBN 978-1-4521-1739-3 (hardback)
1. Knitting—Patterns. I. Title.
  TT825.R6333 2013
  746.43'2—dc23
                    2013004056

Manufactured in China

MIX
Paper from
responsible sources
FSC® C104723
www.fsc.org

Designed by Allison Weiner
Typeset by DC Typography

10 9 8 7 6 5 4 3 2 1

Chronicle Books LLC
680 Second Street
San Francisco, California 94107
www.chroniclebooks.com

To my grandmother Norene Diegelmann, who taught me how to knit when I was a little girl. I am forever grateful that you shared your passion with me, for it has now become mine.

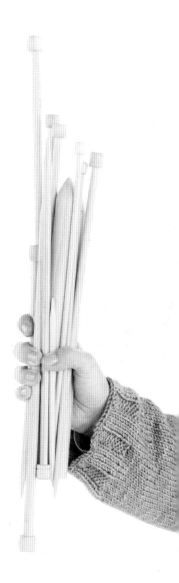

CONTENTS

Tank Top edging?

POM POM BEANIE: garter or stockinette

INTRODUC-
TION

The first time I held a pair of knitting needles, I was a teenager, clueless about what to do with them and what they were capable of creating. Thankfully, my grandmother introduced me to knitting and enthusiastically took the time to teach me the craft. As a child, I remember her getting lost in her knitting for hours, and I admired the time and effort she put into her work, from delicate baby garments for the newest members of the family to felted bags for the more fashionable ones in the bunch. I was intrigued by the challenge of making something so intricate from scratch, so I continued to watch and learn.

Between my busy adolescence and only seeing my grandma a few times a year, my progress was very slow; in fact I didn't pick up a pair of needles for about ten years. When I finally brought knitting back into my life, it went from a hobby to a small business in a matter of months. It started during my final year of college when a few of my girlfriends fell in love with a knitted headband I had made for myself. I decided to take on a few custom orders for fun, word spread, and a few orders quickly turned into one hundred. It was then that I realized there was a large market for affordable and fashionable knitwear. I jumped at the opportunity to design more pieces that stylish women would want to incorporate into their wardrobes.

After college, I decided to open up an online store and knit full time. The knitting and fashion market embraced me with open arms, and the shop's success inspired me to push my skills and designs even further. I hired professional photographers to capture images of my products,

I researched knitwear in fashion, I sold my designs at craft fairs, and I met with other knitters to try to become more integrated into the knitting community. All of this helped move me forward as a knitter and as a small business owner.

As I continue to knit, I find myself wanting to refine my design process even more. Beyond aspiring to be an educated and talented knitter, I strive to shine as a knitwear designer. This takes time, dedication, and learning from your mistakes. With each piece, we learn more about knitting and how we function best when working within the craft. We learn what colors and textures we gravitate toward, what designs we're favoring, and even which stitches appeal to us most.

The fifteen projects in this book will challenge and strengthen your skills by using a variety of different fibers, stitches, needles, and construction methods. From small accessories to more involved garments, I chose a unique batch of projects that are engaging for any knitter, new or experienced. This book also gives a visual glimpse into my design process, from the initial kernel of inspiration for a project through its rewarding finish. You'll see snapshots of the details that inspired me, early sketches used to solidify my ideas, and the textures, colors, prints, and patterns that got my creative juices flowing. As any knitter knows, the design process is a very personal one that is a direct reflection of your taste and creative eye. My inspiration may provide you with entirely different project ideas from the ones I have showcased here. If that happens, run with it—the point is to look at the world around you, gather inspiration, learn how you work best, and make every project your own.

To grow as a designer and a maker of things, it's also important to think outside the knitting box. There are so many beautiful materials you can use to enhance your projects, and I encourage you to do so. Throughout the book, you'll see numerous ideas for using other materials in your pieces; adding a leather pocket to your vest or dip-dyeing a tank top can help you see the possibilities in designing fully functional, one-of-a-kind items. Plus, these small additions can be adapted and applied to many of the other projects in the book.

My hope is that with each peek into my design vision, you will have more insight into your own creative process and can build the confidence to dream up projects from scratch. Knitting is such a vast and diverse craft: it always leaves room for improvement, innovation, and improvisation. I offer these words of encouragement to you as you work through this book and as you move forward as a knitter!

BASIC TOOLS & YARN

You only need a few tools to knit gorgeous pieces. Stock up on the essentials, and you'll work through all these projects with ease. Also, some of the projects incorporate nonknitting materials—from colorful dyes to suede and leather—that will challenge your developing sense of design. In this way, you'll have the opportunity to grow as a crafter and garment maker.

TOOLS

Knitting Needles
You can buy knitting needles of various sizes for each project or you can invest in a set of needles that has everything you will need: circular, straight, and double-pointed.

Measuring Tape
I like the vinyl type of measuring tape with fiberglass strands that won't stretch or deform, allowing you to achieve consistent measuring when working with garments or soft fabrics.

Metal Ruler
The hard, straight edge of a metal ruler is handy when working with materials like leather and suede.

Scissors
I recommend getting a small pair of sharp scissors or snips for yarn and thread, a pair of extra-sharp textile scissors, and a pair of general crafting scissors you can use for paper. You will be working with a range of materials in these projects, so you'll need different scissors to accommodate them.

Stitch Holders
These helpful holders keep live (active) stitches off the needle temporarily while they aren't being worked in the pattern. Leftover lengths of yarn from other projects work just fine for marking spots in your knitting or as stitch holders.

Stitch Markers
These small, plastic or metal rings slip onto your knitting needle and mark a certain spot in your pattern. They are often used to mark the end of a round when knitting in the round, and to indicate certain points in a pattern.

Straight Pins and Safety Pins
A straight pin is a thin needle-like pin used to fasten pieces of cloth together. A safety pin has a clasp with a guard on the end to hold and cover the point.

Tapestry Needle, Embroidery Needle, and Sewing Needle
A tapestry needle is a long sewing needle with a large eye and a blunt tip and is used to sew knitted pieces together. It's sometimes called a darning needle or a yarn needle. An embroidery needle, also known as a crewel needle, has a sharp point and an elongated eye

for easier handling of multiple threads and thicker yarns. It is used for projects where piercing through the fabric is necessary. Sewing needles are used for general hand sewing and are built with a sharp point and round eye.

YARN

Selecting a yarn to work with can be the hardest yet most exciting part of each project. Since there are so many beautiful fibers out there to choose from, it's difficult to know where to begin. There are two ways I like to approach this process. You can design the piece first and then search for a yarn that fits its specifications or you can let a selected yarn dictate how the piece is designed from the very beginning. The majority of my inspiration comes from color and beautiful palettes, so I typically start out by searching for a yarn that catches my eye, and then I begin designing. One thing to remember when selecting a yarn is that there's a wide range of fibers that all have their own unique properties. Some of the projects in this book require the use of a specific fiber to yield the desired result. As you work through the projects in the book, take a moment to educate yourself on all of the yarns that are used.

Wool

Sheep's wool is very warm yet lightweight, it's resilient, and it has a natural elasticity that helps knitted pieces keep their shape. There is a variety of different sheep breeds whose fleeces are spun into knitting yarn. Some sheep have very fine, soft fleece: Merino is a popular example. Others have coarser, more rugged fleeces used to create yarns that are perfect for a long-wearing outer garment. When subjected to heat, agitation, and temperature changes, wool (and most other animal fibers) will turn into felted fabric. This is great if you want to create a felted piece, but if you don't, remember to wash your knits gently by hand in lukewarm or cool water and lay them flat to dry.

Some wool yarns are put through a chemical process that renders them machine washable. These yarns are labeled "superwash" and are perfect for items like socks or children's garments. The superwash process takes away some of the wool's elasticity and softness, so there is a trade-off.

Other Animal Fibers

Aside from sheep's wool, yarn can be spun from the hair of many animals, including alpacas, llamas, goats, rabbits, camels, and musk oxen. Most of these are considered luxury fibers because they are rare, more complicated to process, and therefore more expensive. These fibers can be incredibly soft and warm and are perfect for special accessories like hats and scarves. They tend to be less elastic than wool, so be cautious before creating a large piece of alpaca or cashmere, and knit several sample swatches to see how the yarn works up.

Plant Fibers

Cotton, flax, and hemp are also used to create yarns. Plant fibers are cool and crisp, and make a good choice for comfy summer T-shirts and sweaters. Plant fibers are heavier than wool and have minimal natural elasticity, so they can be a little harder on your hands to work with.

Synthetic Fibers

A variety of synthetics—acrylic, polyester, polyamide, rayon, viscose, and Lycra to name a few—are commonly used in today's yarns. If acrylic makes you think of cheap rainbow-colored drugstore yarn, it's time to take another look! There is a large range of textures and styles that allows you to broaden your creative opportunities.

ABBREVIA-
TIONS &
TERMS

KNITTING ABBREVIATIONS

beg begin(s), beginning

BO bind off (cast off)

CC contrasting color

CO cast on

dec decrease(s), decreasing

dpn(s) double-pointed needle(s)

inc increase(s), increasing

K or **k** knit

k2tog knit 2 stitches together as 1 stitch (right-slanting decrease)

k3tog knit 3 stitches together as 1 stitch (right-slanting decrease)

kfb knit front and back increase: Knit the next stitch through the front loop but do not drop the stitch from the needle; knit the same stitch through the back loop (tbl), then drop the stitch from the left needle.

kwise knitwise; as if to knit

M1L make 1 left-slanting increase: Insert left needle under the horizontal strand between stitches from front to back; knit this stitch through the back loop.

M1R make 1 right-slanting increase: Insert left needle under the horizontal strand between stitches from back to front; knit this stitch through the front loop.

MC main color

P or **p** purl

pm place marker

pwise purlwise; as if to purl

rem remaining

rep repeat

RS right side

sl slip. Slip stitches purlwise, unless pattern specifies otherwise.

s2kp (centered double decrease): Slip 2 stitches as if to k2tog, k1, pass the 2 slipped stitches over the stitch just knit.

sm slip marker

st(s) stitch(es)

ssk slip, slip, knit (left-leaning decrease): Slip 2 stitches, 1 at a time, as if to knit. Insert left needle into these 2 stitches from left to right and knit them together.

tbl through back loop

tog together

WS wrong side

w&t wrap and turn: Take yarn to opposite side of work (if you're on the knit stitch, bring yarn to the front, if you're on the purl stitch, bring yarn to the back), slip next stitch from left to right needle purlwise, return yarn to working side, then slip stitch back from right to left needle purlwise. The remaining stitches are unworked. Turn and continue working.

wyib with yarn in back

yo yarn over

SELECTED KNITTING TERMS

As you work your way through the book, these terms will be used. Please refer to this section if you need assistance.

Cable Cast-On

1. Place a slipknot on the left-hand needle.
2. Insert right-hand needle into this stitch and knit it, but *do not* slide the stitch off.
3. Transfer this newly made stitch onto the left-hand needle.
4. Insert the right-hand needle between the first and second stitch on the left-hand needle. Wrap the yarn and pull it through, creating a new stitch.
5. Transfer this newly made stitch onto the left-hand needle.

Repeat steps 4 and 5 until the appropriate number of stitches have been cast on.

Garter Stitch

When knitting back and forth, knit every row. When knitting in the round, knit the right-side rows and purl the wrong-side rows.

Negative ease

When a pattern has negative ease, the finished item should fit snugly.

Positive ease

When a pattern has positive ease, the finished item should fit loosely.

Provisional Cast-On

Step out your favorite technique here, or find one online or in another book.

Three-Needle Bind-Off

1. Divide stitches evenly between 2 needles as described in the pattern.
2. With right sides together and wrong sides facing out, hold the 2 needles together in the left hand with the needle tips pointing to the right.
3. Insert a third needle of a similar size knitwise into the first stitch on the front needle then the first stitch on the back needle, and knit these 2 stitches together.
4. Repeat step 3 so that there are two stitches on the right-hand needle.
5. Bring the outside stitch on the right-hand needle over the inside stitch on the right-hand needle to bind off.

Repeat steps 3 and 4 until 1 stitch remains on the right-hand needle. Cut yarn and pull it through the last stitch to secure, unless pattern specifies otherwise.

Whipstitch

1. Begin by threading a tapestry needle with your yarn and tying a knot in the end. Push the needle up through the top layer of the fabric only. This hides the knot between the two pieces of fabric.
2. Wrap the thread around the edge of the fabric and push the needle from the bottom up through both layers of fabric so that it exits in the same place as your first stitch.
3. Wrap the thread again around the edges of the fabric, and push it up through both layers of fabric. Push it through the same hole as before and angle the needle so that it comes out about $\frac{1}{8}$ in/3 mm from the first stitch. The thread between each stitch will be hidden within the two fabrics.
4. Push the needle up through both fabrics, directly underneath where the second stitch comes out of the top layer of fabric. Again, angle the needle so that it comes out $\frac{1}{8}$ in/3 mm away from the second stitch.

Continue these steps until you have reached the end of the area that you need to sew. Make sure that the final stitch ends straight up and down and not angled to the side. Push the needle through the bottom of this stitch for the second time but only go through the bottom layer of fabric. Tie a knot so that it's hidden between the two layers of fabric, as in step 1. Weave in the end of the thread.

THE DESIGN PROCESS

Designing knitwear can be intimidating to those who have never taken a stab at it, but believe me, you can do it. You'll need to learn about the materials you're working with, develop a basic understanding of fashion and design, and, of course, recognize your own creative point of view. If you approach it slowly, systematically, and patiently, you'll be well on your way to creating beautiful garments. The first step is simple: pay attention to the world around you. Spend time looking at garments you love and ask yourself what you like about them. Pinpointing the things you do and don't like will help you determine what you want to make.

As you start out, you will quickly become more in tune with the smaller individual parts that go into a piece as a whole. Shapes, silhouettes, patterns, texture, color combinations—there are many details to consider. When you can break down a garment into its individual elements and see them as separate decisions, you'll begin to understand the freedom and options you have when designing. Keep in mind that everyone interprets what inspires them differently. Your vision is the result of your background, interests, experiences, and surroundings. These elements all influence your decisions in a really beautiful, one-of-a-kind way, so I encourage you to embrace your own point of view as you make your way through this book and each of your own projects.

Designing involves a process of planning and testing, because all of the fibers available to work with have different qualities that affect the results. Following is a basic run-through of what's involved in designing knitwear. Some designers do all of these steps, while others prefer to skip a step or two and dive right in. Either way, you'll find that it takes a bit of trial and error as you establish your preferred way of working.

INSPIRATION

Doing visual research always kick-starts my energy and excitement for designing a new project. It's good to have a variety of visual resources for creative stimulation. Keep in mind that knitting inspiration can just as easily come from nonknitted materials and garments. If you were only looking at knitting books and websites, you would simply be inspired by what's already been done. Branch out and allow your eyes to sift through what's new and fresh, in all sorts of fields, and you'll come up with innovative and unique ideas. As soon as I began to open up my creative vision to unrelated items, I was amazed at how I was able to bring different directions into my projects. Some of my favorite ideas have come from unexpected places. For example, last year I fell in love with a watercolor artist who primarily paints and sketches in fashion. She inspired me to explore hand-dyeing a knitted piece so that it had a soft, painterly feel.

My favorite go-to spot for instantaneous inspiration is Pinterest, an online platform for sharing and organizing visual content. By following people within this platform who align with my taste, I am exposed to art, photography, fashion, graphic design, architecture, and other eye candy that I might not find on my own. I also regularly visit blogs, fashion magazines, vintage shops, flea markets, and bookstores. I have a favorite local bookstore that is packed with visual stimulation. Whether it's from a graphic design book, an architecture magazine, or an illustrated magazine, good ideas always come from a visit.

As you dive into this early stage of the design process, it's good to keep a sketchbook for all of your thoughts that will be flying in. I usually have three or four notebooks in use at one time in which I make lists, jot down ideas, and sketch. The amount of pens and markers I have in my bag at all times can be pretty humorous. I also love to take quick snapshots with my phone of things I see that are interesting. The perk to keeping these sketchbooks and visual reminders is that you will always be able to refer to and build on them as you grow and expand as a designer. I enjoy going back and looking at my ideas from previous projects, to get some perspective on how my taste and creative process has changed over time.

SKETCHING

Once you've filled your head and sketchbooks with ideas, it's time to choose a few and put pen to paper. By drawing out a design, you will begin to break the piece down and discover the particular decisions you need to make. Do you want edging? Where would you like the seams to meet? What will the neckline shape be? It's easy to focus on the main style of the piece and overlook the details, so loosely sketch and find those little areas that need attention. I'm spontaneous and freewheeling when I sketch. I draw many versions in all different types of pens and markers, hoping that one in particular will really grab my attention. When that happens, I focus on the distinct elements that set it apart and really play those up. For example, when I was working on the Balloon

Sweater (page 133), I knew I wanted the arms to have a unique shape. As soon as I started playing around with the wrists and their proportions, I got really excited and knew that I had found the element that would keep me energized and interested in the project.

Beyond just sketching out my ideas, I also like to bring in other materials such as paint or cut paper to experiment with. For this book, I incorporated spray paint into a lot of my sketching and brainstorming. I had never used this method before and really loved the outcome. The soft texture of the spray paint gave my sketches an airbrushed effect. Working with this new medium allowed me to look at my ideas in a different light. Constantly changing your methods of sketching and becoming inspired—trying new things and pushing the limits—will keep you moving forward as a designer.

SWATCHING

Turning your sketches into a pattern isn't as simple as plugging some numbers into an equation. The next step to making a design come to life is getting to know your fibers through test swatching. In this process, you knit up a small amount of yarn using all the basic elements you plan to use for your pattern—your chosen stitch, needle size, and yarn type. As you begin to make decisions, ask yourself questions: What fiber would you like to work with? What mood do you want your color palette to create? Do you want the texture of the stitches to be bold or soft? If you need help making these decisions, flip through yarn options on a website or go to a local yarn shop and browse their fiber and needle selections. My favorite go-to resources when I am stuck are my stitch books. I have a handful of them that are filled with hundreds of different stitch ideas. Flipping through them reminds me how much I love certain stitches or inspires me to try something new. By walking yourself through all of this, you're one step closer to dreaming up what your piece will look like.

Test swatching will slowly narrow your ideas down until you have determined the perfect elements for your project. As I become more experienced and familiar with the fibers that are available, I have built up a list of favorites. I like to save all of my swatches and label them to use as references when making decisions for other projects. Keep in mind that this is the time to experiment and have fun; you can't mess up. As you begin to knit, make sure that your swatches are no smaller than 4 by 4 in/10 by 10 cm. The larger the swatch of fabric, the more accurate your project will be, so don't hesitate to invest the time into making a big swatch. It's also important to wash and dry your finished swatch so that you are completely aware of how that yarn behaves when it's knitted up into a fabric. Some will grow substantially in length or width, or if you are using a machine-washable yarn, you might find that it shrinks. Knitting an entire garment requires a lot of time and effort, so doing your homework assures a result that you'll be pleased with.

Even if you like the yarn and stitch pattern you've chosen, take time to experiment with needle size too. Sometimes everything works out perfectly and you move through all these steps smoothly and successfully. Other times you'll hit roadblocks and have to adjust. If you knit a swatch too loosely, for instance, and you want the finished design to be much tighter, go down a needle size or two and make a new swatch. Be patient and keep working until you're 100 percent pleased with the result, because you will be using your final swatch when it comes time to draft out the dimensions of your piece. For example, if you want the length of a sweater to be 21½ in/54 cm and your swatch's gauge is 13 stitches and 26 rows per 4 in/10 cm, you can do the math to see how many rows you need to knit to achieve that specific length. The same thing goes for width and the number of stitches that you'll need to cast on. You can figure out almost everything from your swatches, so take advantage of making them often and big.

NOW IT'S TIME TO KNIT.

Since all knitters work and organize their projects differently, you'll discover how you prefer handling this final step. No matter what route you take, you will be using your final swatch measurements that resulted from a combination of a stitch pattern, needle size, and yarn choice. I prefer to plan the pattern out solely by using the measurements my swatch yielded.

When casting on, I refer to how many stitches per 1 inch/2.5 centimetres my swatch has, the measurements I decided on when designing the piece, and then I do the math. For instance, if my T-shirt measures 19 in/48 cm wide and my washed swatch tells me I am knitting 4 stitches per 1 in/2.5 cm on size 9 needles, then that tells me to cast on 76 stitches. This part of the process is when trial and error plays a big role. It may take a handful of tries to get a sleeve width right or a neckline looking exactly as you imagined it, and that's typical; I almost never get it right on the first try, and I've come to regard these challenges as good lessons learned. I take notes on everything that happens while I am figuring out a pattern—good and bad—so that I can know exactly what I did and learn from it. I have found that with every piece I make, I take away something new. The notes give me encouragement when I can't figure something out and get frustrated. I'm reminded that by not giving up, I am going to become an even better knitter.

Let's get started!

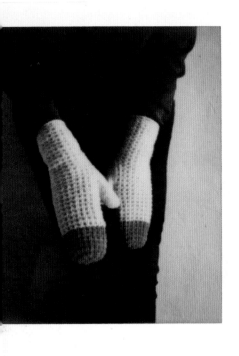

PROJECTS

MITTENS WITH A POP

COLOR BLOCKING FRENZY

Perk up your winter accessories by knitting these perfectly fitted mittens. Your hands will not only make a bold statement, but they'll also stay super-warm with this extra-fine wool. I put a playful design focus on the tips of the mittens because they are the most visible parts. Then, I approached the design with my two favorite things in mind, color and trend. The neutral bottom halves and bright color-blocked tips allow you to adapt these to your wardrobe by choosing whatever color palette you like.

SKILL LEVEL
Intermediate

SIZE
S(L)

FINISHED MEASUREMENTS
Circumference: 7(8½) in/18(21.5) cm
Length: 15(16) in/38(40.5) cm

YARN
Worsted
Manos del Uruguay Maxima Semi-Solid (100% extra fine merino wool; 219 yd/200 m per 100 g): 2590 Natural (MC), 1 skein; M2175 Hot Pink (CC), 1 skein

NEEDLES
US 7/4.5 mm set of 4 double-pointed needles (dpns), *or size needed to obtain gauge*

NOTIONS
2 stitch markers (of contrasting colors)
Tapestry needle

GAUGE
20 sts and 36 rows per 4 in/10 cm in waffle stitch, unblocked

SPECIAL STITCH
Waffle Stitch Pattern
Worked in the round over an even number of stitches:
Round 1: Knit.
Round 2: Knit.
Round 3: *K1, sl1 pwise wyib; repeat from * to end of round.
Round 4: *P1, sl1 pwise wyib; repeat from * to end of round.
Repeat Rounds 1-4 for waffle stitch pattern.

INSTRUCTIONS

(make 2)

Body

Starting at the wrist cuff edge, with MC, CO 36(44) sts and divide them evenly onto 3 dpns.

Join to work in the round, being careful not to twist. Place marker (pm) to indicate beginning of round.

Work the 4 rounds of waffle stitch a total of 14(18) times. The mitten measures approximately 6½(7) in/16.5(18) cm.

Thumb Gusset

Round 1: K2, pm, work in waffle stitch to end of round.

Round 2: M1L, k2, M1R, sl marker (sm), work in pattern to end of round—38(46) sts.

Round 3: K across thumb stitches, sm, work in pattern to end of round.

Round 4: M1L, k to marker, M1R, sm, work in pattern to end of round—40(48) sts.

Rounds 5, 7, and 9: K to marker, sm, work in pattern to end of round.

Rounds 6, 8, and 10: M1L, k to marker, M1R, sm, work in pattern to end of round—46(54) sts.

Round 11: K to marker, sm, work in pattern to end of round.

Round 12: Sl 12 thumb sts onto scrap yarn, remove second marker, CO 2 sts using cable cast-on (see page 14), work in pattern to end of round—36(44) sts.

Fingertips

If you would like your mittens to be one solid color:

With MC, repeat 4 rounds of pattern 14(18) more times. The mitten now measures approximately 14(15) in/ 35.5(38) cm.

To change color for the fingertips:

With MC, repeat 4 rounds of the pattern 8(10) more times. The mitten now measures approximately 11(12) in/ 28(30.5) cm.

Join CC and work 4 rounds of pattern 6(8) more times. The mitten now measures approximately 14½(15½) in/ 37(39) cm.

Shape fingertips for both styles:

Round 1: *K1, s2kp, repeat from * around—18(22) sts.

Round 2: Knit.

Round 3: *S2kp; repeat from * around (for larger size, end k1)—6(8) sts.

Break yarn and thread through remaining 6(8) sts. Pull gently to close.

Thumb

Transfer the 12 thumb sts from scrap yarn onto dpns.

With MC, k12, pick up and k4 sts from the body of mitten, pm to indicate beginning of round—16 sts.

Knit 15 rounds.

Next round: *K2tog; rep from * around— 8 sts.

Break yarn and thread through remaining 8 sts to close.

FINISHING

Fasten off. Weave in ends with the tapestry needle.

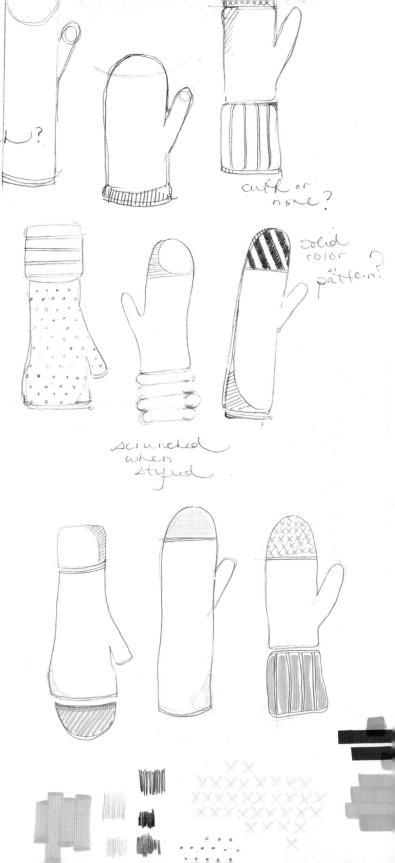

design inspiration

I knew I wanted something more than just a single-color mitten, so I started exploring how to bring in multiple colors. I asked myself what areas of the mitten were the best for a color change or unique detail. I decided that the fingertips and wrist allowed the most space for design freedom. I could play around with the shape of the tips: they could be round, oval, or squared off. They could fold back and button so that the fingers could be exposed. For the wrists, I could play around with the length of the mittens: Would it look good if they were extra long and scrunched up? Or short and trim? Ultimately, I decided that the tips, whose round, enclosed fingertips distinguish mittens from gloves, would be the focus of my design. The first pair I knitted had neon-pink tips and was a huge success, so I chose them for the first project in the book. Sometimes a design works out perfectly and you get it right the first time.

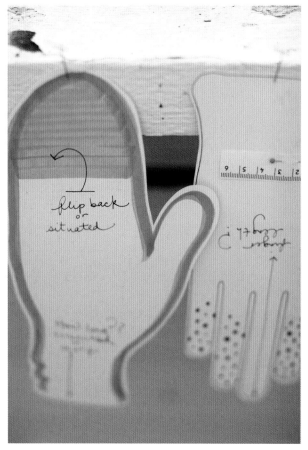

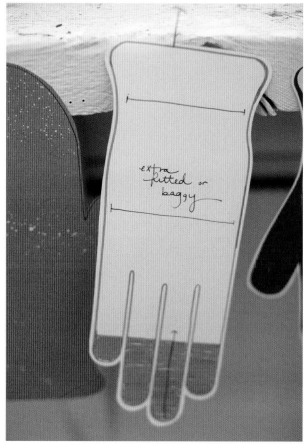

yarn & stitch

I chose Manos del Uruguay Maxima Extra Fine Merino Wool because the line not only offers rich, bright colors but the yarn is incredibly soft, making it the perfect fabric for a cozy winter item. The graphic waffle stitch was chosen to accompany the bright colors to create an overall extra bold look.

trial & error

The main challenge for this item was making a seamless shift between yarn colors. I hadn't considered how my stitch pattern would act when I got to this part of the project, but thankfully, the waffle stitch yields a clean transition and it looked wonderful. Since I also wanted to play around with wrist/cuff length, I decided I wouldn't make a decision on the cuffs until I could try them on. I knitted several mittens with different cuff lengths and stitch treatments to decide which combination I liked best. I could have just done swatches, but since this was a smaller piece, it made sense to invest the time so I could see how the finished items would look.

CHUNKY COWL

MIX & MATCH

Oversized and warm, this cowl will quickly become your statement piece on chilly days. I've knit the cowl out of two kinds of yarn, to bring in some subtle color accents, but there are so many creative directions you can take. Play with different added materials like string, ribbon, and fabric—the options are endless. Style your cowl loosely over a sweater, or pile it on top of your winter coat—either way, you're bound to stay cozy in its multiple layers of soft alpaca.

SKILL LEVEL
Beginner

SIZE
One size

FINISHED MEASUREMENTS
Circumference: 50 in/127 cm
Width: 9 in/23 cm

YARN
Sport
Blue Sky Alpacas Bulky Alpaca
   (50% alpaca/50% wool; 45 yd/41 m
   per 100 g): 1002 Silver Mink (MC),
   5 skeins
Bombay by Fil Katia (100% mercerized
   cotton; 251 yd/230 m per 100 g):
   4 pinks and reds (CC), 1 skein

NEEDLES
US 17/12.75 mm straight needles, *or size
   needed to obtain gauge*

NOTIONS
Tapestry needle

GAUGE
8 sts and 9 rows per 4 in/10 cm in
   pattern, unblocked
NOTE: Matching gauge is not crucial in
   this project.

INSTRUCTIONS

Starting at one end, and holding the MC
and CC together as if they were one yarn,
CO 23 sts.

Row 1: *K2, p2; repeat from * to last 3 sts,
k2, p1.

Repeat this row until piece measures
50 in/127 cm, or desired length.

BO.

FINISHING

With wrong sides together, using a
tapestry needle threaded with your yarn,
whipstitch (see page 14) the cast-on and
bound-off rows together.

Fasten off. Weave in ends.

how large?

layer and stack

design inspiration

yarn & stitch

When designing this piece, I wanted to go really big, so the cowl would feel like it's wrapped around me like a blanket. The main question was just how large should I actually go with it? I wanted the cowl to be extremely dramatic but still wearable. First I tackled the size, and then I chose the thickness, or weight, of the yarn as well as how many times I wanted it to wrap around.

While sifting through Pinterest, I came across an image of a knitted blanket that was made out of the thickest yarn I'd ever seen. When it came time to choose yarn for this project, my thoughts went directly to that one. Why not use the same approach and go extra thick! I began sorting through bulky-weight yarns and came across Blue Sky Alpacas, which offered a beautifully rich jewel-tone palette. I considered doubling up two different kinds of yarn that would complement each other, create an interesting mix, and yield thicker results. I ended up experimenting with this idea a lot and using it. For the stitch, I wanted a ribbed pattern that would give the cowl a striped effect. I consulted my stitch book and found the perfect one that would create a texture that showcased this thick yarn.

trial & error

When I made my first test swatch, I realized that the ribbed pattern was going to come out vertical in the piece, but I thought it would look best if the ribs were horizontal, so when the cowl was wrapped around my neck, the stripes would flow in the wrapped direction. I modified the design by using straight needles instead of knitting in the round, to get that effect. But using straight needles created its own challenge: having two ends made from very thick yarn that needed to be seamlessly connected. Sometimes, you have to be flexible and test new solutions to make the design work.

RAINY-DAY VEST

LAYERING WITH LEATHER

This fall staple is not your average vest. Its wide collar and silhouette are accentuated by the yarn's marbled effect and the hand-sewn leather pocket. When I started to design the piece, I put all my focus on the large collar, which folds back naturally and works like its own separate layer. I then chose the seed stitch, which produces a beautiful texture and weight that make the vest a pleasure to layer over your favorite collared blouse or patterned dress.

SKILL LEVEL
Intermediate

SIZE
XS(S, M, L)
Fits bust circumference: 30(34, 38, 42) in/ 76(86, 96.5, 107) cm

FINISHED MEASUREMENTS
Bust circumference: 34(38, 42, 46) in/ 86(96.5, 107, 117) cm with collar overlapped
Length: 23½(24, 24½, 25) in/ 60(61, 62, 64) cm

YARN
Worsted
Madelinetosh Tosh Vintage (100% superwash merino wool; 200 yd/ 183 m per 100 g): Graphite, 5(6, 6, 7) skeins

NEEDLES
US 7/4.5 mm circular needle, 32 in/81 cm long, *or size needed to obtain gauge*
US 7/4.5 mm straight needle

NOTIONS
Stitch markers, 4 of one color (MC) and 2 of contrasting color (CC)
Tapestry needle
Stitch holder

LEATHER POCKET
Scrap paper and pencil
Metal ruler
Straight pins
Safety pins
1 piece of thin leather about 6 in/15 cm square
Cutting mat
X-ACTO knife
Small awl to punch tiny holes in thin leather
Small hammer
Thin sewing needle
Nylon or linen thread of coordinating color
Thimble

SPECIAL STITCH
Seed Stitch
Work in the round over an odd number of stitches:
All rows: *K1, p1; repeat from *, k1.
In all subsequent rows, knit the purls and purl the knits to create the seed st pattern.
NOTE: When you decrease, work the decrease as a knit, but otherwise maintain the seed st pattern, knitting purls and purling knits.

GAUGE
20 sts and 40 rows per 4 in/10 cm in seed stitch, unblocked

INSTRUCTIONS

Body

Starting at the bottom edge, using circular needle, cast on and place markers as follows: CO 39 (42, 46, 50) sts, place first main color (MC) marker, CO 1, place second MC marker, CO 39 (42, 46, 50), place first contrasting color (CC) marker, CO 97 (107, 117, 127), place second CC marker, CO 39 (42, 46, 50), place third MC marker, CO 1, place fourth MC marker, CO 39 (42, 46, 50)— 255 (277, 303, 329) total sts rem.

MC markers indicate where you will make your center front decreases; CC markers indicate your side decreases.

Work 11 rows in seed st pattern.

Row 12: *Work to 1 st before first MC marker, remove both markers, s2kp, replace markers on either side of the decreased stitch; repeat from *, then continue in seed st to end of row—4 sts decreased.

Work 11 rows in seed st.

Row 24: Work to 1 st before first MC marker, remove both markers, s2kp, replace markers on either side of the dec st, work to 2 sts before CC marker, k2tog, sl marker (sm), ssk, work to 2 sts before CC marker, k2tog, sm, ssk, work to 1 st before MC marker, remove both markers, s2kp, replace markers on either side of this decreased stitch, work in seed st to end—8 sts decreased.

Repeat these 24 rows 5 more times— 183(205, 231, 257) sts.

Work even until piece measures 15½ in/ 39 cm, or desired length to underarm, ending with a RS row.

Divide for armholes:

Next row (WS): *Work to 3(5, 6, 7) sts before first CC marker, BO 6(10, 12, 14) sts; rep from * then work to end— 79(85, 93, 101) sts for the back and 46(50, 57, 70) sts for each front. You may place the sts for the Back and for the Left Front on stitch holders, or simply leave them on the needle until they are needed.

Right Front

Shape the armhole and neck as follows, and at the same time dec 1 st every 12th row.

Next row (RS): Work to end.

Next row (WS): Work 2 sts, ssk, work to end.

Repeat the last 2 rows 2(3, 4, 5) more times.

Continue in seed st, dec 1 every 12th row as set, until armhole measures 7 in/ 18 cm (all sizes). End with a WS row.

Neck shaping:

Next row (RS): Work in seed st pattern.

Next row (WS): Work to last 5 sts, s2kp, work 2 sts in seed st.

Repeat the last 2 rows 5(6, 8, 12) more times while continuing to dec 1 at each marker every 12 rows—25(25, 27, 30) sts. Armhole measures approximately 8(8½, 9, 9½ in/20(21.5, 23, 24) cm.

Place sts on a stitch holder.

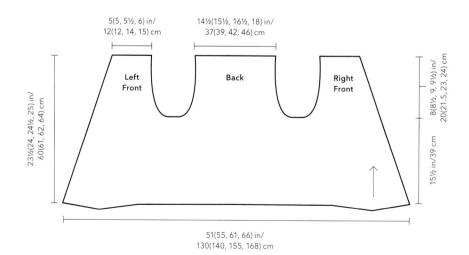

5(5, 5½, 6) in/
12(12, 14, 15) cm

14½(15½, 16½, 18) in/
37(39, 42, 46) cm

Left
Front

Back

Right
Front

23½(24, 24½, 25) in/
60(61, 62, 64) cm

8(8½, 9, 9½) in/
20(21.5, 23, 24) cm

15½ in/39 cm

51(55, 61, 66) in/
130(140, 155, 168) cm

Left Front

Join yarn at armhole with RS facing.

Next row (RS): Work to end.

Next row (WS): Work to last 4 sts, k2tog, work 2 sts in seed st.

Repeat the last 2 rows 2(3, 4, 5) more times.

Continue in seed st, dec 1 every 12th row as set, until piece measures 7 in/18 cm (all sizes). End with WS row.

Neck shaping:

Next row (RS): Work in seed st pattern.

Next row (WS): Work 2 sts, s2kp, work to end in seed st.

Repeat the last 2 rows 5(6, 8, 12) more times while continuing to dec 1 at each marker every 12 rows—25(25, 27, 30) sts. Armhole measures approximately 8(8½, 9, 9½) in/20(21.5, 23, 24) cm.

Place sts on holder.

Back

Next row (RS): Join yarn and work in seed st.

Next row (WS): Work 2 sts, ssk, work to last 4 sts, k2tog, work last 2 sts.

Repeat the last 2 rows 2(3, 4, 5) more times—73(77, 83, 89) sts.

Work even in seed st until back measures the same as the two fronts.

FINISHING

Fold garment so shoulders are aligned and right sides are touching.

Using the three-needle bind-off (see page 14) to join the 25(25, 27, 30) sts of one shoulder, BO in seed st pattern across the 23(27, 29, 29) neck sts, and then use the three-needle bind-off to join the other shoulder.

Fasten off. Weave in ends.

Adding a leather pocket:

1. Create a paper template for the pocket, to help you cut the leather in the correct size and shape. Use a ruler to draw a square onto the paper. Mine measures 3 in/7.5 cm, but feel free to make yours larger or smaller. Design and draw in the bottom point of your pocket. If you want to avoid using a ruler, you can trace the back pocket from your favorite jeans. Cut out the template.

2. Pin the template onto the vest where you'd like it to be sewn. Then try the vest on to see how it looks when worn. When you are satisfied, mark the template's location with safety pins.

3. Lay the piece of leather on the cutting mat and place the paper template on top. Using your metal ruler as a straight edge, carefully cut the leather with an X-ACTO knife.

4. Using the awl, punch tiny holes about ¼ in/6 mm apart along the side and bottom edges of the pocket. You may need to tap the awl with a small hammer so that you puncture the leather all the way through. Work on the cutting mat or another work surface (like an old phone book) so you won't harm your table.

5. Place the leather pocket on the marked spot of the vest and hold it in place. Using a needle and thread, and a thimble to protect your backup finger, whipstitch (see page 14) it onto the vest. Fasten off the thread and weave in the ends.

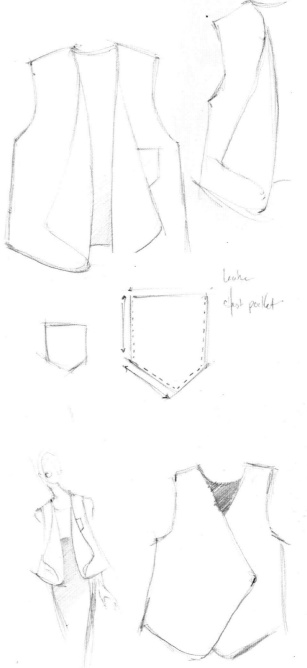

design inspiration

I have never been a big fan of vests so I wanted to challenge myself to make a version that I'd want in my wardrobe. After thoroughly researching vests within men's and women's fashion, I chose to design a piece inspired by menswear. The key to this was focusing on the masculine shapes and proportions and then translating them into a chic and sophisticated finished item. I designed a less tailored but still feminine piece, developed the collar shape, and added a small leather pocket. Working with leather is always an adventure—there are so many different options to choose from. Should I use a light camel color or a dark, rich chocolate brown? Should the piece be extra thick or thin? I loved going through scrap bins and finding pieces to experiment with. Planning the size and shape for the pocket was important so I didn't waste any leather. I made a ton of paper templates before I committed to one.

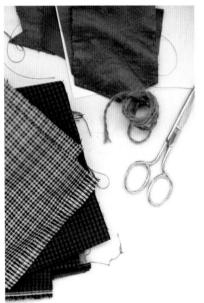

yarn & stitch

The hand-dyed yarn gives the vest warmth as well as a natural worn look of a vintage piece you've had for years. I chose the seed stitch with this yarn because when it's knitted up, it looks a lot like tweed, a fabric often used in menswear.

trial & error

The length of the piece was my main challenge. The first version I made was rather short, so I lengthened the design. I wanted the vest to fall longer and be a layering piece that would work with a variety of outfits. So I added 6 in/15 cm to the bottom of the second vest, and it looks perfect.

COZY COLLAR

PREPPY CASUAL

This project was inspired by a big fluffy wool collar I found at a flea market. It sits on your shoulders and offers the perfect amount of extra warmth when you don't need a full-blown scarf wrapped around you. Layer it over your favorite jacket or chic dress to enhance your look with a decorative, stylish element.

SKILL LEVEL
Intermediate

SIZE
One size

FINISHED MEASUREMENTS
Width: 6 in/15 cm
Length: 34 in/86 cm

YARN
Bulky
Tahki Yarns Maya (100% cotton; 108 yd/ 99 m per 100 g): black, 6 skeins, *or other yarn, or combination of yarns, to achieve the suggested gauge*

NEEDLES
US 15/10 mm straight needles, *or size needed to obtain gauge*

NOTIONS
Tapestry needle

GAUGE
9½ sts and 16 rows per 4 in/10 cm in garter stitch, working three strands together, unblocked

INSTRUCTIONS

Collar

Starting at one end, and holding three
  strands of yarn together, CO 4 sts.

Row 1 (RS): K1, kfb, knit to last 2 sts,
  kfb, k1.

Row 2 (WS): Knit.

Repeat last two rows 4 more times—
  14 sts.

Knit 28 rows even.

Shape collar using short-row shaping:

Row 1: K10, w&t, knit to end.

Row 2: K6, w&t, knit to end.

Row 3: K2, w&t, knit to end.

Row 4: Knit across, picking up all wraps
  and knitting them together with the sts
  they wrap.

Row 5: Knit across.

Repeat short-row shaping, Rows 1–5,
  4 more times.

Knit 6 rows even.

Repeat short-row shaping, Rows 1–5,
  5 more times.

Knit 28 rows.

Next row (RS): K1, k2tog, knit to last
  3 sts, ssk, k1.

Next row (WS): Knit.

Repeat last two rows 4 more times—4 sts.

BO.

FINISHING

Fasten off. Weave in ends with the
  tapestry needle.

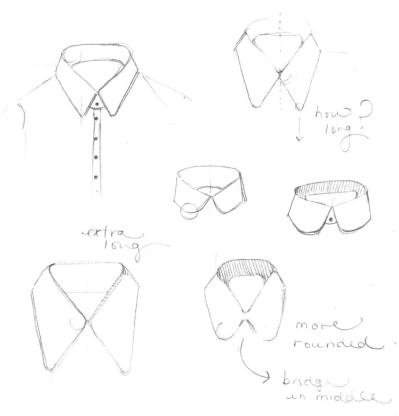

how long?

extra long

more rounded

bridge in middle

design inspiration

At first, I wanted this piece to be like a necklace or a delicate accessory made out of lace-weight yarn. I was attempting to knit a collar that resembled one from a dress shirt or blouse, so it could sit on your shoulders, wrap around your neck, meet in the back, and enclose with a button. This turned out to be difficult and time consuming, so I changed my game plan and went bigger. I basically took the same concept, enlarged it, and adjusted a few design details so it could become the centerpiece of an outfit rather than a delicate detail.

yarn & stitch

I was initially inspired by vintage wool collars that are layered over coats in the winter: They sit on your shoulders, adding an extra layer of warmth. Those collars influenced many of the design decisions I made, and I chose a thick and thin yarn that creates a chunky, uneven texture.

trial & error

When I was developing my original idea, I knit with lace-weight yarn and size 0 needles. I attempted to design a shape that resembled a dress shirt collar and would be worn similar to a necklace. I quickly decided that the miniature approach wouldn't work, because the shape I wanted was too difficult to achieve on such a small scale. I was glad that I tried working that small, but most likely I won't choose to work on a mini scale in the future. After all, you should enjoy the process of making a piece, not just the end result. You have the freedom to decide what you want to make but also how much time you want to spend on it and how challenged you want to feel.

TWISTED TURBAN

WRAP IT UP

This quick and easy turban-inspired headband is great for a fashionable look on the go. The twist on top gives it more character than a scarf or headband, and the layers can be wrapped in a variety of ways and will keep your ears super-warm. Whether you're having a messy hair day or need that final accessory to polish your outfit, this versatile piece will become one of your favorites.

SKILL LEVEL
Beginner

SIZE
One size

FINISHED MEASUREMENTS
Length (before closed into a loop):
   50 in/127 cm
Width: 6½ in/16.5 cm

YARN
Worsted
Cascade Yarns 220 (100% Peruvian
   Highland wool; 220 yd/201 m per
   100 g): 7818 Blue Velvet; 1 skein

NOTE: This piece is knit loosely with worsted weight yarn to give it the desired drape.

NEEDLES
US 9/5.5 mm, *or size needed to obtain
   gauge*

NOTIONS
Tapestry needle

GAUGE
15 sts and 18 rows per 4 in/10 cm in
   stockinette stitch, unblocked

INSTRUCTIONS

Body
Beginning at one end, CO 25 sts.
Work in stockinette st until piece
  measures 50 in/127 cm.
BO loosely.

FINISHING
Using a tapestry needle, stitch the cast-on
  and bound-off edges together, being
  sure to keep the strip untwisted.
Fasten off. Weave in ends.

TO WEAR
Hold the loop in both hands, twist it
  twice, and double it over. Then pull
  it over your head and style your hair.
  The photo shows how I like to wear it,
  but you can twist and wrap it in many
  different ways.

design inspiration

I was originally inspired by the shape of a traditional turban. I wanted to make a modern version that would be a great accessory for women. I focused on creating a headband that could be twisted and styled in multiple ways. To allow for this variety of styles, I had to determine the right amount of material to work with while also achieving a snug fit.

twist for knot

knot: how large?

yarn & stitch

I wanted the stitch to create a flat, smooth texture, like a silk scarf or cotton fabric. The piece is incredibly simple to make, and stockinette stitch worked perfectly. To balance out the accessory's simplicity, I used a bright colored yarn.

trial & error

This piece is a long skinny rectangle that is connected to make a loop. My first design was twisted first and then closed up: by the time you had it on your head, there were too many twists so it was too bulky. I discovered that it is more clean and neat when you connect it first and then twist it in a desired style.

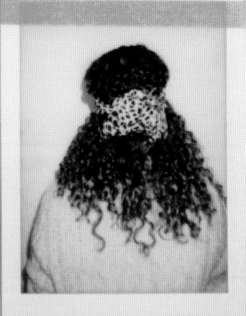

OMBRÉD TANK TOP

FADING FUN

Knitting doesn't have to be confined to fall and winter projects if you don't want it to. Inspired by lightweight and delicate knits, this piece can be worn in either cool or warm weather. Introducing dye—to create a faded ombré effect—into the equation kicks the challenge up a technical notch but also vamps it up visually. Wear this vibrant, personalized piece to the beach as a cover-up or layer it with a jacket.

SKILL LEVEL
Intermediate

SIZE
XS(S, M, L)
Fits bust circumference:
30(34, 38, 42) in/76(86, 96.5, 107) cm

FINISHED MEASUREMENTS
Bust circumference: 26(30, 34, 38) in/
66(76, 86, 96.5) cm
Length: 23(23½, 24, 24½) in/
58(60, 61, 62) cm
NOTE: The top will grow quite a bit during the dyeing and drying process. The numbers in the pattern account for this, but if you try it on before you get it wet, the fit will only be approximate.

YARN
DK
Knit Picks Bare Swish DK (100% merino wool; 246 yd/225 m per 100 g):
Natural, 2(2, 3, 3) skeins

NEEDLES
US 10.5/6.5 mm circular needle, 24 in/
60 cm long, *or size needed to obtain gauge*
US 7/4.5 mm circular needle, 24 in/
60 cm long
US 7/4.5 mm circular needle, 16 in/
40 cm long

NOTIONS
2 stitch markers (of contrasting colors)
Stitch holders

DYEING
NOTE: Do not use any utensils that you cook with. The dye is toxic when consumed.
2 quarts very hot water
1 large bowl or small bucket (3 qt/2.8 L or larger capacity)
1 jar of Jacquard Acid Yarn Dye (net weight ½ oz/15 g)
1 cup/240 g salt
¼ cup/60 ml white vinegar
Large mixing spoon

1 disposable clothes hanger
1 disposable hanger with clips (like for pants or skirts)
1 packet large clothespins
1 pair rubber gloves
1 small spray bottle
Plastic trash bags or drop cloth
1 roll plastic wrap (the kind you use to seal food items)
Microwave oven

GAUGE
16 sts and 22 rows per 4 in/10 cm in stockinette stitch, unblocked on larger needles
18 sts and 18 rows per 4 in/10 cm in stockinette stitch, blocked
NOTE: After knitting a swatch, wet it and hang vertically to dry, weighted with some clothespins. This will help you assess your blocked gauge, and whether your finished top will fit.

INSTRUCTIONS

Body

Beginning at the bottom edge, with the smaller, 24-in-/60-cm-long, circular needle, CO 232(272, 308, 340) sts.

Join to work in the round, being careful not to twist. Place first marker (pm) to indicate the beg of the round.

Round 1: Knit.

Round 2: Purl.

Repeat Rounds 1 and 2 four more times.

Switch to the larger circular needle and k2tog to end of round—116(136, 154, 170) sts total.

Work even in stockinette st until piece measures 14 in/35.5 cm, or desired length to underarm, bearing in mind that piece will grow in length approximately 2½ in/6 cm after dyeing and drying.

Shape armholes:

Set-up round: K58(68, 77, 85), pm, k to end of round.

Next round: K to 4(6, 6, 8) sts before second marker, BO 8(12, 12, 16) sts, k to 4(6, 5, 8) sts before first marker, BO 8(12, 12, 16) sts.

You will now be working back and forth on the 50(56, 65, 59) *back* stitches only. You can place the front stitches on scrap yarn or just leave them on the cable of your circular needle.

Next row (RS): K2, k2tog, k to last 4 stitches, ssk, K2.

Next row (WS): Purl.

Repeat last 2 rows 3(4, 6, 6) more times—42(46, 51, 55) sts.

Work even until piece measures 3(3½, 4, 4½) in/7.5(9, 10, 11) cm wide, ending with a WS row.

Shape neck:

Next row: K11(12, 13, 15), BO 20(22, 25, 25) sts, k to end.

You will now work on the 11(12, 13, 15) sts for the left shoulder only.

Next row: Purl.

Next row: K2, k2tog, k to end.

Repeat the previous 2 rows 1 more time—9(10, 11, 13) sts.

Work even in stockinette stitch until armhole measures 6½(7, 7½, 8) in/16.5(18, 19, 20) cm, then put these sts on a holder.

Join yarn to work right shoulder with WS facing.

Next row: Purl.

Next row: K to last 3 sts, ssk, k1.

Repeat the previous 2 rows 1 more time—9(10, 11, 13) sts.

Work even in stockinette st until armhole measures 6½(7, 7½, 8) in/16.5(18, 19, 20) cm, then put these sts on a holder.

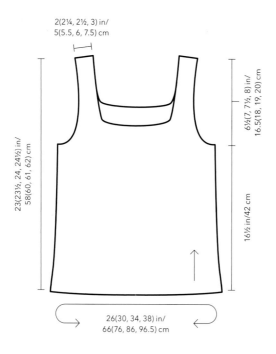

2(2¼, 2½, 3) in/
5(5.5, 6, 7.5) cm

23(23½, 24, 24½) in/
58(60, 61, 62) cm

6½(7, 7½, 8) in/
16.5(18, 19, 20) cm

16½ in/42 cm

26(30, 34, 38) in/
66(76, 86, 96.5) cm

Front

You will now work the front sts: Join the yarn to the 50(56, 65, 59) front sts, with right side facing.

Next row (RS): K2, k2tog, k to last 4 stitches, ssk, k2.

Next row (WS): Purl.

Repeat these 2 rows 3(4, 6, 6) more times—42(46, 51, 55) sts.

Shape neck:

Next row: K11(12, 13, 15), BO 20(22, 25, 25) sts, k to end.

You will now work on the 11(12, 13, 15) sts for the right shoulder only.

Next row: Purl.

Next row: K2, k2tog, k to end.

Repeat the previous 2 rows 1 more time— 9(10, 11, 13) sts.

Work even in stockinette st until armhole measures 6½(7, 7½, 8) in/ 16.5(18, 19, 20) cm, then put these sts on a holder.

Join yarn to work left shoulder with WS facing.

Next row: Purl.

Next row: K to last 3 sts, ssk, k1.

Repeat the previous 2 rows 1 more time— 9(10, 11, 13) sts.

Work even in stockinette st until armhole measures 6½(7, 7½, 8) in/ 16.5(18, 19, 20) cm. Leave these sts on the needle.

FINISHING

Turn tank inside out and use the three-needle bind-off (see page 14) to join the shoulder seams.

Fasten off.

Armhole edging:

With RS facing and using the smaller (16-in/40-cm) circular needle, pick up and knit approximately 6 sts per 1 in/2.5 cm around one armhole. The exact number of sts you pick up is not important.

Work 3 rows in garter stitch (knit all rows).

BO loosely.

Fasten off.

Work second armhole edging in the same way.

Neck edging:

With RS facing and beginning at one shoulder seam, pick up 6 sts per 1 in/ 2.5 cm around the neckline.

Place marker to indicate beginning of round.

Next row: Purl.

Next row: Knit.

Next row: Purl.

BO loosely.

Fasten off.

Weave in ends.

Dyeing your tank top:

NOTE: You do not need to block your tank top before you start dyeing. The piece will stretch a bit during the dyeing process, but the measurements given in the pattern account for this. I recommend that you test the dyeing process on a large swatch before dyeing your finished piece.

1. Completely saturate the tank top with cold tap water for about 10 minutes. Gently press down on your yarn while it is in the water to ensure that all the air bubbles have been removed. Then gently squeeze out the extra moisture with a towel so it's damp, not soaking wet.

2. To make the dye bath, pour 2 qt/2 L of very hot water into the bowl.

3. Pour in about half the jar (¼ oz/7 g) of dye.

   NOTE: This is double the strength recommended on the package.

4. Pour in 1 cup/240 g of salt.

5. Pour in ¼ cup/60 ml of vinegar.

6. Stir the mixture until everything has dissolved.

7. Once you've made the dye bath, make sure the bowl's edges are clean so no extra dye gets on your knitted piece. Now it's time to dip! (Before you attach your damp tank top to the hanger, consider where you will be hanging it while it soaks in the dye bath.)

CONTINUED

8. To achieve the effect shown, clip the tank upside down to the hanger with clips so that the upper part will be submerged to about 3 in/7.5 cm below the neckline. (It's up to you which end of the tank top you would like to soak in the dye. For this project, I dyed the straps and let the fading effect go toward the bottom.) Add extra clothespins to keep the piece from stretching while hanging. It's important that it hangs straight to assure an even dip-dyeing line and fading effect.

9. Slowly lower the tank top into the dye bath and hang for 30 to 45 minutes. Throughout the soaking process, make sure to keep the area around the dye line damp. Use a small spray bottle of water to keep the area properly saturated. You want it to be wet enough so the dye can naturally and slowly move upward as it soaks into the yarn.

10. After 30 to 45 minutes, remove the tank top from the dye bath and hanger and squeeze out any excess dye. Make sure to wear rubber gloves so you don't stain your hands. Do not touch above or near the dye line because you might mess up the smooth fading effect. Once you're done gently squeezing out the excess dye, wash your gloves so they are free from any color.

11. Flip the tank top right-side up and hang it from a regular hanger. Make sure to place your trash bag or drop cloth below your piece so dye and water doesn't drip or splash on anything. As the piece hangs to dry, the dye will slowly run and create an ombré effect. I recommend doing this during a window of time that allows you to monitor the dye as it spreads. If it isn't spreading at all, use the spray bottle to evenly dampen the dye line. Be careful not to wet the piece too much because this will cause the dye to run unevenly; a little goes a long way.

12. Once you're happy with the results, take the piece down and lay it on a plastic trash bag. This will stop the spreading of the dye and will provide an area for you to prep your piece for the microwave.

13. Carefully wrap your tank top up in plastic wrap. This is going to keep the moisture in while it heats up in the microwave. It's important that your piece doesn't dry out or burn. The dye is not fully set yet so be sure not to let it touch any of the undyed parts of the garment.

14. Put the wrapped tank top in the microwave. Heat the tank top for 1-minute intervals until the piece is thoroughly heated all the way through. Make sure to let it cool down for 1 minute between each heating interval and check that it isn't drying out. The trick is to get the whole piece hot, but not heat it for so long that the fabric gets dry. The actual heating time required will vary somewhat depending on the volume of water that the tank top still contains and the actual wattage of your microwave. Hint: Put a glass of water in the microwave with your piece to help distribute the heat.

15. Allow the yarn to cool, and then remove the tank top from the plastic wrap.

16. Carefully start rinsing the tank top in warm water. This will remove any excess dye that did not set in the microwaving process. You don't want any of that excess color to spread into the clean area of your tank, so dunk it in the rinse water a little past the dye line. This allows the undyed area to stay outside of the rinse water and untouched by any excess dye. Continue rinsing and changing the rinse water until your rinse water is clear.

17. Lay the piece out to dry.

design inspiration

One of the first knitted patterns I ever made was a tank top in light pink cotton yarn. I felt such a sense of accomplishment when I finished that project that the impression stuck with me. When designing pieces for this book, I was inspired to create my own tank top pattern. I wanted

something light and airy for summertime, just like my pink cotton one. I also wanted it to have a simple, traditional fit. In thinking about adding something extra-special to the design, I turned to all of the current ombréd designs that I'd been seeing. I decided to dye the finished

piece to achieve that same beautiful fading effect. I had never hand-dyed yarn before, so I did a lot of research. I am a huge fan of color, so the visual idea of a bright dye running down a stark white tank top got me excited about designing this unique piece.

yarn & stitch

Since I wanted to work with dye, I chose a yarn that would take color well and would be lightweight; Bare Swish DK Wool met all the requirements. I ordered extra because I knew I was going to be making swatches and testing different dye methods. When considering which stitch to use, I thought it needed to be smooth and flat so the dye could evenly run down the piece.

trial & error

To perfect the dyeing part of the process, I started out by making tons of long, skinny, rectangular swatches, so the dye could run and I could accurately see results. I dyed the swatches with different colors and methods. For something that is going to be washed on a regular basis, the dye needs to be as fixed to the fibers as possible. If this doesn't happen, the dye will bleed and run as soon as it is immersed in water. The challenge was finding a method that would set the dye but also enable it to bleed and actually create the ombré effect. I knew this would be possible after reading up on the process of microwave dyeing. By wrapping up the dip-dyed piece and zapping it in the microwave, the heat and the water in the piece completes the process of setting the dye. It was a bit nerve-racking putting something I had spent hours on into the microwave, but it worked and came out beautifully ombréd and rich in color. My advice to you as you work through this project is to do as many tests and practice rounds as you possibly can. There is nothing worse than ruining a piece that you spent lots of time and money on.

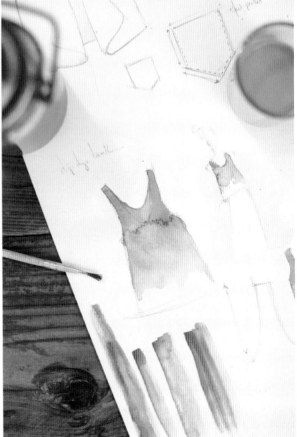

BIG BOW HAIR CLIP

SEEING STRIPES

Occasionally, you have to bust out the girliest accessory of them all—the bow. This oversize, striped bow hair clip is quick and easy to make and instantly changes the personality of an otherwise average look. Instead of creating a traditional bow that ties and loops, I decided to design it as a flat piece and pinch it in the middle so the bow has a lot of movement without being too bulky or heavy. Pair this super-femme hair clip with whatever hairstyle you rock best.

SKILL LEVEL
Beginner

SIZE
One size

FINISHED MEASUREMENTS
Before pinched into a bow: 10 in/25 cm long and 5 in/12 cm wide

YARN
Worsted
Cascade Yarns 220 (100% Peruvian Highland wool; 220 yd/201 m per 100 g): 8885 Dark Plum (MC), 5 stripes, around 24 yd/22 m; 7809 Periwinkle (CC), 4 stripes, around 20 yd/18 m

NEEDLES
US 9/5.5 mm straight needles, *or size needed to obtain gauge*

HAIR CLIP
Small barrette-style, 1 in/2.5 cm long

GAUGE
16 sts and 30 rows per 4 in/10 cm in garter stitch, unblocked

INSTRUCTIONS

Striped Bow

NOTE: When you change colors, do not cut the yarn. Instead, twist the next color of yarn around the previous color (to prevent holes in the finished piece), and carry the unused color up the side throughout the pattern. This prevents having to weave in several ends.

CO 20 sts in MC.

Knit 8 rows.

Drop MC and work in CC.

Knit 8 rows.

Continue knitting, alternating MC and CC to make 8-row stripes, until you have a total of 9 stripes.

BO loosely.

FINISHING

Fasten off. Weave in ends with the tapestry needle.

To create the bow, pinch the rectangle in the center and tie a long piece of MC yarn around the center in a tight knot to hold it in place. Do not cut this yarn once you have tied the knot.

Wrap the yarn around the center until it starts to take shape as the bow's center.

Once your knot is almost to its desired thickness, open up the hair clip, slip the backside of the clip through the center of the knot (making sure you have positioned it so you can still open and close the clip), and continue to wrap, securing the clip in place.

Fasten off. Weave in ends.

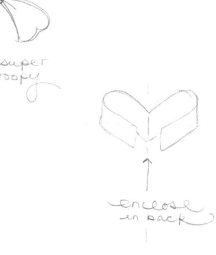

super droopy

enclose in back

design inspiration

The first piece I ever designed was a tiny, incredibly girly knitted headband. When I decided to update the project for this book, I knew I wanted to go bigger to make the piece bolder and more dramatic. Instead of making it a headband, I designed it with a clip so that it had more range for styling—hair up, hair down, or even pinned as a brooch. I started out knitting bows in solid colors and then realized that stripes would be really fun. I went with thicker and bolder stripes, but I also think that thinner, more delicate stripes would look equally eye-catching.

rounded or pointy

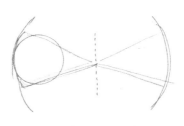

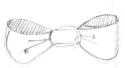

super thin or thick

yarn & stitch

I wanted all the focus of this piece to be on the size and simple shape, not on an elaborate stitch. So I settled on the garter stitch. For yarn, I was drawn to Cascade 220 because the line comes in such a spectacular array of colors. For my stripes, I chose two shades of the same color, creating a pleasing complementary palette.

trial & error

It took me a few times of knitting the entire bow to perfect the size—not too precious but not overwhelmingly large. I also experimented with transitioning between colors when knitting stripes. Did I want to carry the yarn up the side of the piece or cut it every time and have lots of ends to weave in? My main concern was that the piece look clean, so I felt that carrying the yarn up the side would be the best option.

MULTICOLORED CARDIGAN

TONE ON TONE

It's always a challenge to successfully transition your wardrobe to winter as the cold weather approaches. This cardigan maintains its flowy shape even when worn with lots of layers, plus it brings some bright color into a season that tends to be filled with neutrals. When designing this piece, I wanted to take a unique approach. My favorite aspects are the color change, the use of two different stitches paired with a thick edging, and the hand-sewn suede elbow patches. I made a lot of design decisions to achieve the right amount of detail, to make the sweater truly stand out from every other cardigan in your closet.

SKILL LEVEL
Beginner

SIZE
XS(S, M, L)
Fits bust circumference:
  30(34, 38, 42) in/76(86, 96.5, 107) cm

FINISHED MEASUREMENTS
Bust circumference: 35(38, 42, 45) in/
  89(96.5, 107, 114) cm
Length: 22(23½, 24, 24½) in/
  56(60, 61, 62) cm

YARN
Worsted
Sweet Georgia (100% superwash merino
  wool; 200 yd/183 m per 115 g): Glacier
  (MC), 4(5, 5, 6) skeins; Pistachio,
  3(3, 3, 3) skeins

NEEDLES
US 9/5.5 mm circular needle, 24 in/60 cm
  long, *or size needed to obtain gauge*
US 9/5.5 mm circular needle, 16 in/
  40 cm long

NOTIONS
Stitch markers
Tapestry needle
Stitch holder

ELBOW PATCHES
Scrap paper and pencil
Straight pins
Safety pins
1 piece of thin suede (about 12 in/
  30.5 cm by 12 in/30.5 cm)
Cutting mat
Scissors
Small awl to punch holes
Small hammer
Sewing needle
Coordinating thread

GAUGE
20 sts and 26 rows per 4 in/10 cm in
  stockinette stitch and in cross-over
  stitch, unblocked
NOTE: Some knitters may need to use
  different needle sizes to obtain the
  same gauge over both stitch patterns.

SPECIAL STITCH
Cross-over Stitch
Worked flat, or turning at the end of a
  row on a circular needle:
Row 1 (RS): K1, *yo, k2, pass the yo over
  the 2 sts just knit, repeat from * to last
  st, k1.
Row 2 (WS): Purl.
Repeat rows 1 and 2 for cross-over st
  pattern.

INSTRUCTIONS

Back

Starting at bottom edge, with the longer (24-in/60-cm) circular needle and MC, CO 88(96, 104, 112) sts. Do not join; this piece is worked back and forth.

Next row (RS): K6, *p4, k4; rep from * to last 2 sts, k2.

Next row (WS): P6, *k4, p4; rep from * to last 2 sts, p2.

Repeat the previous 2 rows until piece measures 2 in/5 cm.

Switch to stockinette st and work even until piece measures 23(23½, 24, 24½,) in/58(60, 61, 62) cm.

Leave sts on holder or spare needle.

Right Front

Starting at the bottom edge, with longer circular needle and MC, CO 42 (46, 52, 56) sts.

Work in cross-over st pattern until piece measures 17(17½, 17½, 18) in/43(44.5, 44.5, 46), ending with a WS row.

Neck shaping:

Next row (RS): K1, yo, k2tog, pass the yo over the k2tog (2 sts on right-hand needle), work in cross-over st to end.

Next row (WS): Purl.

Next row (RS): K1, yo, k2tog, k1, pass the yo over the 2 sts just worked, work in cross-over st to end.

Next row (WS): Purl.

Repeat the last 4 rows 15(15, 17, 17) more times—26(30, 34, 38) sts.

Work even until piece measures 23(23½, 24, 24½) in/58(60, 61, 62) cm.

Left Front

Beginning at bottom edge, CO and work as for Right Front until it is time to shape the neck.

Neck shaping:

Next row (RS): Work in cross-over st to last 3 sts, yo, ssk, pass the yo over the st just knitted, k1.

Next row (WS): Purl.

Next row (RS): Work in cross-over st to the last 4 sts, yo, k1, ssk, pass the yo over the 2 sts just knitted, k1.

Next row (WS): Purl.

Repeat these last 4 rows 15(15, 17, 17) more times—26(30, 34, 38) sts.

Work even until Left Front matches Right Front.

Join Fronts and Back

With right sides facing, use three-needle bind-off (see page 14) to join the 26(30, 34, 38) shoulder sts, BO the 36(36, 36, 36) back neck sts, use three-needle bind-off to join the sts for second shoulder.

Lay sweater flat, measure down 7(7½, 8, 8½) in/18(19, 20, 21.5) cm from shoulder on front and back, and place marker (pm). Repeat on the opposite side. Use the tapestry needle to mattress stitch the side seams from the hem to the marker.

Sleeves (work both the same)

Starting at the underarm (RS), and using the shorter circular needle, join CC to pick up and knit 70(76, 80, 86) sts around armhole, pm.

Joining to work in the round, work in stockinette st, and at the same time, decrease every 12th (10th, 8th, 6th) row 7(10, 12, 15) times as follows: k1, k2tog, k to last 3 sts, ssk, k1—56 sts.

Work even until piece measures 16 in/40.5 cm or 2 in/5 cm short of desired sleeve length.

Cuff (work the same for both cuffs)

Work in K4, p4 rib around.

Repeat this rib round until the cuff measures 2 in/5 cm.

BO loosely.

FINISHING

Fasten off. Weave in ends.

Block as desired on a flat surface.

Create and attach suede elbow patches:

1. Create a paper template for the elbow patch. This will help you cut the suede in the correct size and shape. Use a pencil to draw an oval template that is 3 in/7.5 cm wide and 5 in/12 cm tall. (Feel free to make your patches smaller or larger than I've suggested.)

2. Decide where you would like to place
   your elbow patches. Pin the template to
   a cardigan sleeve and try the sweater on
   to see how the patches will look when
   the garment is being worn. Try resting
   your elbow on your desk while striking
   the pose of an avuncular professor to
   get the location just right. Once you've
   decided on the placement, mark both
   spots with safety pins.

3. Lay out your piece of suede on the
   cutting mat. Pin the template to
   the suede and cut out a patch, using
   a sharp pair of scissors. Repeat to
   cut two patches.

4. Using the awl, punch tiny holes about
   ¼ in/6 mm apart around the edge of
   a patch. You may need to tap the awl
   with a small hammer so that you punch
   through the leather. Work on the cutting mat or some other work surface
   so you won't harm your table. Repeat
   for the second patch.

5. Place a suede patch on one sleeve in
   the marked location. Using the needle
   and thread, whipstitch (see page 14)
   the patch in place. Repeat for the
   second patch.

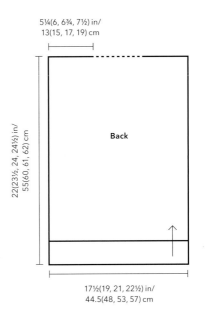

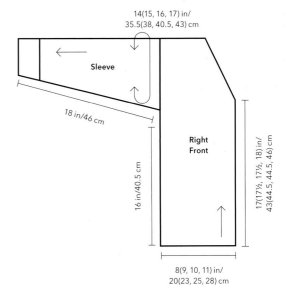

design inspiration

This piece is traditional-prepster with a twist. The color palette makes it happy and loud while its shape and the suede patches keep it grounded. The dropped shoulder and lack of buttons separates it from other cardigans. Whenever I wear a cardigan, I never button it up, so I made the decision to leave buttons off this one. When I committed to the dropped shoulder, I knew that calling it out by the abrupt color transition would highlight this feature in a graphic way—it reminds me of an athletic letterman jacket.

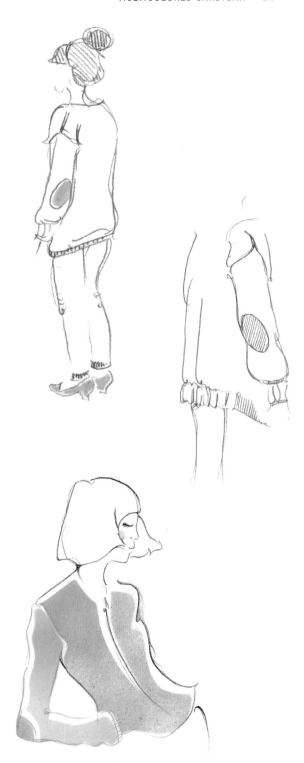

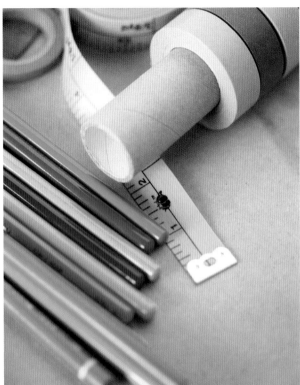

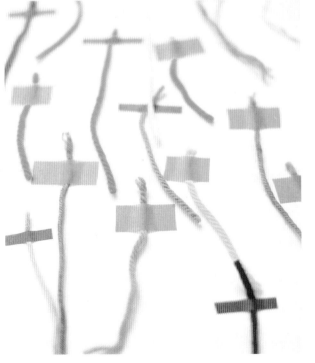

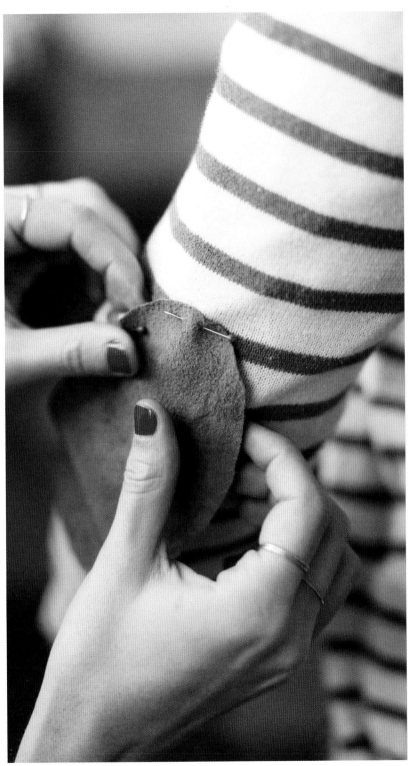

yarn & stitch

Each section of the cardigan was treated differently by changing up the colors and stitches used. The stitches and different trim treatments keep your eyes moving over the piece, taking in all the intriguing details. I was careful to keep the colors and textures well balanced so the cardigan is fun without being too busy.

trial & error

The first time I sewed on the suede patches, the positioning did not work at all. They were uneven and not very close to the elbows. I thought I would be able to eyeball it but I quickly realized I needed to be more precise than that. That's how I came up with the professorial system in the pattern, which helps you mark the placement and get it right.

LAZY-DAY TEE

PATTERN PLAY

Nothing beats that perfect T-shirt—the one you've had for years that's well worn from all the love you've given it. With this project, I've translated that idea into a comfy knitted shirt. The soft cotton and baggy fit emulate that coziness we all crave on lazy days, and the simple embroidered pattern mimics the graphic or words on your favorite T-shirt. Feel free to play around with your embroidery— consider knitting a subtle pattern or phrase that has particular meaning to you. When you're done, you'll have a casual and customized shirt all your own.

SKILL LEVEL
Intermediate

SIZE
XS(S, M, L)
Fits bust circumference:
   30(34, 38, 42) in/76(86, 96.5, 107) cm

FINISHED MEASUREMENTS
Bust circumference: 34(38, 42, 46) in/
   86(96.5, 107, 117) cm
Length: 23(23½, 24, 25) in/58(60, 61,
   64) cm
This top is designed to be loose fitting,
   so allow 4 to 8 in/10 to 20 cm of
   positive ease (see page 14).

YARN
Both are worsted
Classic Elite Yarns Solstice (70% organic
   cotton, 30% wool; 100 yd/91 m per
   50 g): 2319 Petal, 7(8, 8, 9) skeins
Embroidery yarn: Berroco Comfort
   (50% super fine acrylic, 50% super
   fine nylon; 210 yd/192 m per 100 g):
   9702 Pearl, about 5 yd/4.5 m,
   depending on design

NEEDLES
US 9/5.5 mm circular needle, 24 in/60 cm
   long, *or size needed to obtain gauge*
US 9/5.5 mm circular needle, 16 in/
   40 cm long
1 double-pointed needle, any small size

NOTIONS
Stitch markers
Scrap yarn
Tapestry needle

GAUGE
17 sts and 24 rows per 4 in/10 cm in
   stockinette stitch, unblocked

INSTRUCTIONS

Body

Starting at the bottom edge, with the longer (24-in/60-cm) circular needle and using a provisional cast-on, CO 144(160, 180, 196) sts.

Pm and join to work in the round, being careful not to twist.

Knit 10 rounds.

Purl 1 round.

Knit 10 more rounds.

Slowly pull out the provisional cast-on edge, and, using dpn, k1 cast-on st together with 1 st on your circular needle. Repeat all the way around. Work even in stockinette st on these 144(160, 180, 196) sts until piece measures 15 in/38 cm, or desired length to underarm.

Divide front and back:

K72(80, 90, 98), turn. You will now be working back and forth on these 72(80, 90, 98) sts only (the back).

Back

Continue in stockinette st until the back measures 5(5½, 5½, 6) in/ 12(14, 14, 15) cm from the division of front and back, ending with a WS row.

Shape neck:

Next row (RS): K26(29, 34, 38), BO 20(22, 20, 22) sts, k to end.

You will now be working each shoulder separately.

Right side of neck:

Next row (WS): Purl.

Next row (RS): K2, ssk, k to end of row.

Repeat the last 2 rows 3(3, 4, 4) more times.

Work even on these 22(30, 30, 33) sts until the back measures 7½(8, 8½, 9) in/ 19(20, 21.5, 23) cm from beg of armhole. BO.

Left side of neck:

Rejoin yarn at neck edge.

Next row (WS): Purl.

Next row (RS): K to last 4 sts, k2tog, k2.

Repeat the last 2 rows 3(3, 4, 4) more times.

Work even on these 22(30, 30, 33) sts until back measures 7½(8, 8½, 9) in/ 19(20, 21.5, 23) cm from beginning of armhole. BO.

Front

Rejoin yarn at the underarm with the RS facing and work as for back.

Shoulder Seams

Seam the front and back pieces together at the shoulders.

Sleeves (work both the same)

Using the shorter circular needle and starting at the underarm, pick up and knit 64(68, 72, 76) sts around armhole. Pm and join to work in the round.

Work even until sleeve measures 5(6, 6, 7) in/12(15, 15, 18) cm, or 1 in/2.5 cm short of desired length.

Using a piece of thin scrap yarn and a tapestry needle, thread yarn through the last row worked on the WS, so you know which purl bumps to pick up at the end. Be sure to indicate the first stitch of the round.

Knit 5 rounds.

Purl 1 round.

Knit 5 rounds.

Next round: Being sure to start with the first stitch from both rounds, *pick up 1 stitch from the marked row by inserting the double-pointed needle into the purl bump on the WS, then knit this stitch together with 1 stitch from the circular needle; repeat from * and, at the same time, BO all stitches.

NOTE: You can pick up several stitches at a time with the dpn if you prefer.

Neck Ribbing

With RS facing, join yarn at shoulder and, using the shorter circular needle, pick up and knit 86(86, 96, 96) sts around neck.

Work in k1, p1 rib for 5 rounds.

BO loosely.

FINISHING

Fasten off. Weave in ends with the
 tapestry needle.
Block piece on a flat surface.

Embroider a pattern:

You can copy the embroidery I've done
 here or create your own motif using
 graph paper. You can also find printable
 "knitter's graph paper" free online
 to assist you in planning a custom
 embroidery pattern.

1. Figure out how large you'd like your
 design to be, count up the number of
 stitches you have in a corresponding
 section on the graph paper, then
 sketch out your design. My design
 starts 2½ in/6 cm below the center
 of the neck and extends out from
 there. I made each X 3 sts wide and
 3 sts tall, but you can experiment
 with a variety of sts.

2. Select the contrasting yarn that you'll
 use to embroider with. I recommend
 using a worsted-weight yarn similar to
 the yarn you have used in the T-shirt.

3. To start embroidering each X, put the
 needle in from the wrong side of the
 garment so that when you've finished,
 the embroidery tails are hidden. You
 don't need to cut the yarn between the
 cross stitches if they are close together,
 but it's better to use a separate length
 of yarn if you are in doubt.

4. Once your entire pattern has been
 embroidered, flip the piece inside
 out. You will have 2 tails for each X.
 Loosely tie each pair of tails in a
 knot to secure.

5. Weave in ends.

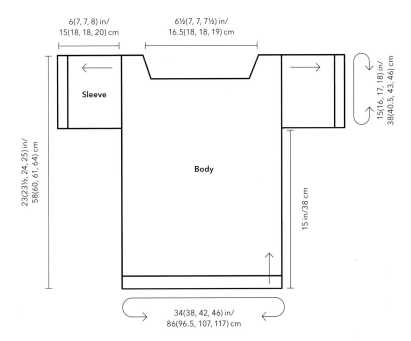

6(7, 7, 8) in/
15(18, 18, 20) cm

6½(7, 7, 7½) in/
16.5(18, 18, 19) cm

Sleeve

Body

23(23½, 24, 25) in/
58(60, 61, 64) cm

15(16, 17, 18) in/
38(40.5, 43, 46) cm

15 in/38 cm

34(38, 42, 46) in/
86(96.5, 107, 117) cm

design inspiration

This garment was inspired by my favorite comfy T-shirts that I never get sick of wearing. My design is a bit heavier and warmer than the ordinary tee, but that just makes it all the more comfortable. With its wide neckline that shows a bit of shoulder, the design is baggy but still stylish. Adding the embroidered design makes it one of a kind, just like your favorite band tee or vintage shirt you got at a flea market.

baggy —o— loose fit

yarn & stitch

I wanted a simple stitch that would both yield a flat, soft fabric and be easy to embroider. The details are in all of the edging, which resembles the traditional seam that you see on T-shirts.

trial & error

The first time around, I made the neckline a bit too wide and the sleeves too long. When I tried the finished piece on, the sleeves pulled the neckline down completely off both my shoulders, making it unwearable. Bringing the neckline in a bit and shortening the sleeves helped resolve the issue.

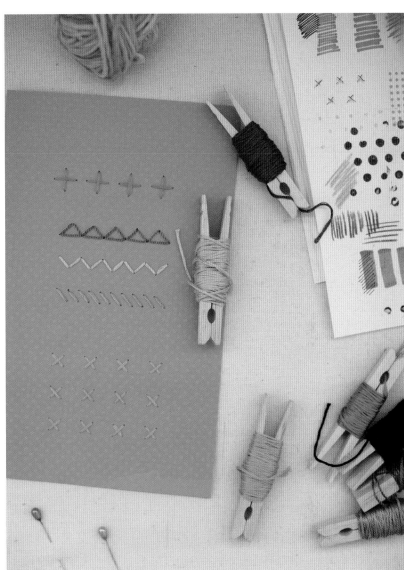

POM-POM BEANIE

SLOUCHY STYLE

This ultimate winter accessory will keep you extra warm while still looking perfectly cool. Knitting the entire hat in stockinette stitch with a bulky yarn creates an eye-catching texture, and adding the large pom-pom on top is a great way to play with proportions—don't be afraid to be adventurous and make it even bigger! Style the beanie pulled down close to your face for a sultry look or pushed back and baggy for a casual feel.

SKILL LEVEL
Beginner

SIZE
One size (fits most adults)

FINISHED MEASUREMENTS
Circumference: 20 in/50.5 cm
Length: 10 in/25 cm (without pom-pom)

YARN
Super Bulky
Blue Sky Alpacas Bulky Alpaca
 (50% alpaca/50% wool; 45 yd/41 m
 per 100 g): 1211 Frost, 2 skeins

NEEDLES
US 15/10 mm circular needle, 16 in/
 40 cm length, *or size needed to
 obtain gauge*
US 15/10 mm set of 4 double-pointed
 needles

NOTIONS
Stitch marker
Tapestry needle

POM-POM
Drinking glass
Pencil
Cardboard, approximately 6 in/15 cm
 square

GAUGE
8 sts and 12 rows per 4 in/10 cm in
 stockinette stitch, unblocked

NOTE: This hat is shown in reverse
 stockinette stitch, but it is worked
 in the round inside out since most
 knitters find it easier to knit than purl.

INSTRUCTIONS

Body

Starting at the bottom edge, CO 40 sts to circular needle.

Join to work in the round, being careful not to twist stitches. Place marker (pm) to indicate beginning of round.

Knit until piece measures 6 in/15 cm.

Begin dec rounds as follows, switching to dpns when needed.

Round 1: *K3, k2tog; repeat from * around—32 sts.

Round 2: Knit.

Round 3: *K2, k2tog; repeat from * around—24 sts.

Round 4: knit.

Round 5: *K1, k2tog; repeat from * around—16 sts.

Round 6: *K2tog; repeat from * around—8 sts.

Cut yarn.

Thread tail through live sts twice and pull snugly to cinch.

Turn hat inside out so that the purl side is showing (as shown here), or if you prefer, leave the knit side out.

Fasten off. Weave in ends on WS with the tapestry needle.

Pom-Pom:

1. Make two cardboard templates to create the pom-pom. Find something round like a drinking glass to trace with your pencil. The pom-pom will be approximately the same size as your cardboard template; mine has a 4-in/10-cm circumference. Trace your circle onto the cardboard twice because you'll need two of them. Draw a circle, approximately $1/3$ in/8 mm smaller, inside each of the larger circles. Draw two lines, approximately $1/2$ in/12 mm apart between the outer and inner circles on each piece. Cut along those lines. In the end, each piece of cardboard should look like the letter C (see top-left photo, page 98).

2. Cut a piece of yarn about 15 in/38 cm long and sandwich between the two pieces of cardboard with the tails hanging out on either side. This will be the piece of yarn that holds the pom-pom together and attaches it to your hat.

3. Wrap your yarn around the sandwiched cardboard templates. As you're wrapping, make sure the template looks like a C at all times. Wrap until you can't see any more cardboard. The more yarn you wrap, the denser your pom-pom will be. I say, the thicker the better: better a puffy pom-pom than a wimpy one.

4. Tie the two loose yarn ends that are sandwiched between the cardboard together into a tight knot.

5. Slip your scissors between the two pieces of cardboard on the outside of the C and begin cutting the yarn all the way around.

6. Remove the cardboard templates from the yarn.

7. Now it's time to attach the pom-pom to your hat. Position it on the top center of the hat and pull both loose ends through to the wrong side with a tapestry needle. Turn your hat inside out. Fasten off. Weave in the ends.

8. Fluff your pom-pom to perfection (give it a trim if it needs one, to even out ends).

← giant pom!

design inspiration

I am a huge fan of hats, so I got really excited when I started this project. I have a growing collection of all different kinds of hats—beanies, cowboy hats, fedoras, costume hats, the list goes on. Accessorizing a look with a hat is such a bold way to take it up a notch, and I wanted this design to be exactly that: bold.

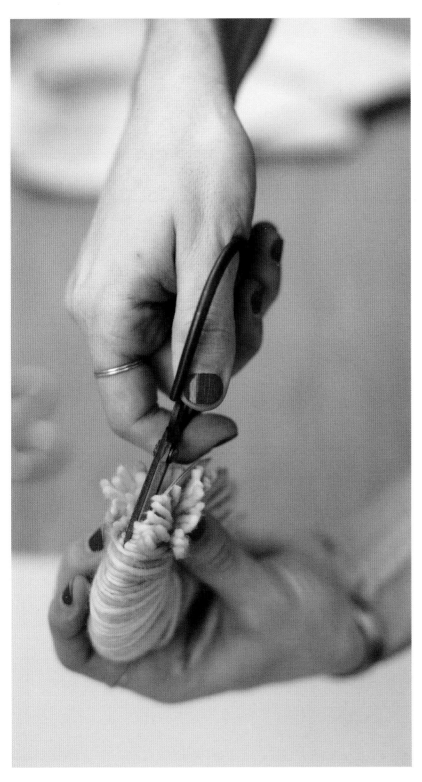

yarn & stitch

The thick yarn I chose makes the stitches dominant and the pom-pom extra fluffy. Any stitch that I used was going to look wonderful in this yarn, so I wasn't too concerned about choosing something flashy or intricate.

trial & error

The main design concern was finding the perfect length for the hat so that it had a bit of a slouch. I envisioned it being worn pushed back a bit and wrinkled up for a baggy, casual feel. I decided on the length by experimenting with my decreasing throughout the pattern. I also spent a ton of time testing out different pom-pom crafting methods. I used kits from craft stores, I made my own cardboard templates like I suggest here, and I even used a more organic approach and let the palm of my hand determine the size. After making way too many pom-poms, I felt like I had an accurate understanding of what yielded the best results.

VINTAGE SUNDRESS

LIGHT LAYERING

Since I've rarely come across a floor-length knitted dress, I thought it would be an exciting and gratifying challenge to try my hand at one. The design knits up incredibly fast and yields a gorgeous feminine shape that can be styled up or down, depending on the occasion. Knit a smaller size for a slim fit that accentuates all of a woman's best features or go larger for a baggy look that can be casually layered and belted. No matter how you plan to style this piece, I guarantee you're going to feel incredibly beautiful in its light and airy design.

SKILL LEVEL
Intermediate

SIZE
XS(S, M, L)
Fits bust circumference:
    32(36, 40, 44) in/81(91, 102, 112) cm

FINISHED MEASUREMENTS
Bust circumference:
    28(32, 36, 40) in/71(81, 91, 102) cm
Length as shown: 58 in/147 cm

NOTE: This pattern makes a very stretchy fabric, so the dress is designed with negative ease (see page 14).

YARN
DK
Louisa Harding Merletto (46% viscose/
    34% polyamide/20% linen; 98 yd/
    90 m per 50 g): Ecru, 6(6, 7, 7) skeins

NEEDLES
US 11/8 mm circular needle, 24 in/60 cm
    long, *or size needed to obtain gauge*

NOTIONS
Stitch markers (of contrasting colors)
Small spray bottle
Tapestry needle

GAUGE
12 sts and 14 rows per 4 in/10 cm in
    stockinette stitch, unstretched

SPECIAL STITCH
Drop Stitch
Worked in the round over even number
    of stitches:
Round 1: Knit, wrapping the yarn around
    the needle twice for each stitch.
Round 2: Knit, dropping extra wraps.
Rounds 3 and 4: Knit.
Repeat Rounds 1-4 for drop st pattern.

INSTRUCTIONS

Body

The dress is worked from the top down, beginning with the neck. You will begin knitting flat, then join to knit in the round after the V-neck is shaped. The beginning of the round will be at the front center.

CO 28(28, 36, 36) sts.

Row 1 (WS): P2, place first marker (pm), p3(3, 5, 5), pm, p18(18, 22, 22), pm, p3(3, 5, 5), pm, p2.

Row 2 (RS): Kfb, kfb, sl marker (sm), kfb, k1(1, 3, 3), kfb, sm, kfb, k16(16, 20, 20), kfb, sm, kfb, k1(1, 3, 3), kfb, sm, kfb, kfb—38(38, 46, 46) sts.

Row 3: Purl.

Row 4: Kfb, *k to 1 st before next m, kfb, sm, kfb; repeat from * 3 more times, k to last st, kfb.

Repeat the last 2 rows 7(7, 9, 9) more times, ending with a RS row— 16(16, 20, 20) sts before the first marker (m) and 98(98, 126, 126) sts total.

Join to work in the round, being careful not to twist. Pm of a contrasting color to indicate beginning of round.

Round 1: Knit.

Round 2: K to 1 st before m, increase before and after each m as set, knit to end of round—8 sts inc.

Repeat last 2 rounds 3(6, 5, 8) more times—130(154, 174, 198) sts.

Create armholes:

Next round: *K to m, remove marker, BO 25(31, 35, 41) sts, remove marker; repeat from *, k to end of round.

Next round: Knit, paying attention to snugging up gaps under the arms.

Knit 1 more round.

Now you will begin using the drop stitch pattern, to create the lacy texture of the dress.

Work the 4 rounds of drop st until piece measures 52 in/132 cm or 6 in/15 cm short of desired length. Do not BO.

FINISHING

Lightly mist the garment with water and hang overnight. The weight of the piece will gently stretch the dress and add a bit to the length. Measure the piece again and work any additional rows to achieve the length you want.

BO loosely.

Fasten off. Weave in ends with the tapestry needle.

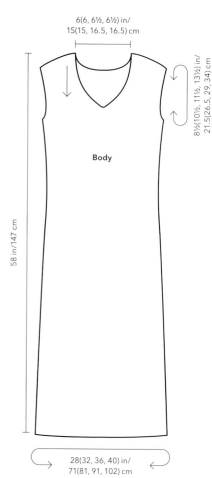

6(6, 6½, 6½) in/ 15(15, 16.5, 16.5) cm

8½(10½, 11½, 13½) in/ 21.5(26.5, 29, 34) cm

Body

58 in/147 cm

28(32, 36, 40) in/ 71(81, 91, 102) cm

This schematic reflects measurements lightly blocked and laying flat. This garment will stretch to fit your body.

design inspiration

Designing a knitted dress was a difficult challenge. There were so many directions I could have gone, so the brainstorming part of the process was a bit overwhelming. I wanted to avoid a heavy look and go toward a slimming and glamorous design. I achieved this by the piece's tight fit, long length, and champagne-colored yarn. I pulled ideas from modern-day dresses as well as vintage designs. I found old photos that were incredibly inspiring, and visits with friends who collect or sell vintage clothing turned out to be a great resource.

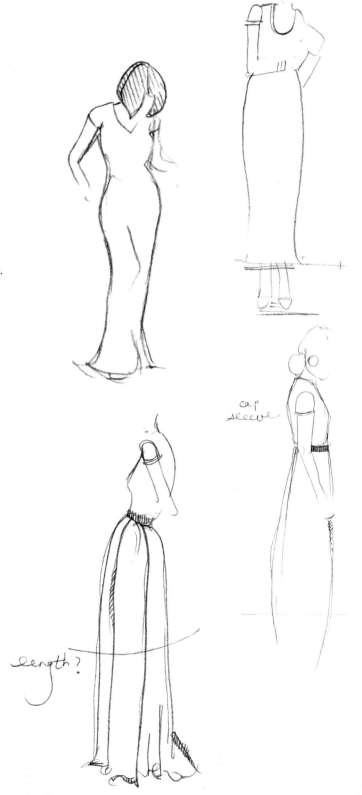

cap sleeve

length?

yarn & stitch

Because this is such a large piece, I wanted to choose a stitch pattern that wouldn't be too time consuming or intimidating to knit. My plan was to use a loose combination of garter stitch and drop stitch—the drop stitch opens up the fabric and creates a sheerness while the garter stitch rows break up the open space, resulting in a striped effect. In the end, the dress knits up quickly and has an intriguing texture. The yarn I chose is perfect for spring and summer garments but was delicate to work with. It was more slippery than most yarns because of a viscose strand twisted in with a matte linen strand. But this was worth it, because it gave the dress a nice sheen, adding to the glamorous feel.

trial & error

My main challenge was figuring out how sheer I wanted to go, so I made extra large swatches to see how the yarn would behave. I knew I wanted the stitch to be open enough to challenge the knitter how to style it but not too sheer so that you're left feeling like you have an insubstantial garment. Even so, both the length and weight were still unknown factors. No matter how large I made my swatches, I knew I wasn't going to be able to truly tell how the yarn would act until the dress was finished and worn. The finished product exceeded my expectations.

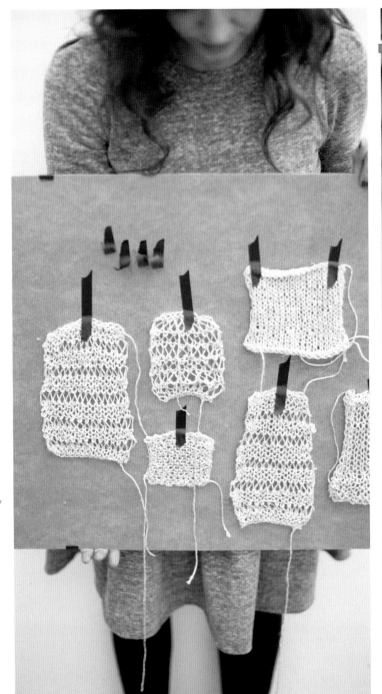

LAID-BACK SHORTS

DRAWSTRING KIND OF DAY

I dreamt up this cozy project because I wanted a pair of shorts that would fit nicely but still give me room to breathe. The finished product has quickly become my new favorite go-to pair of shorts for lazy days in. The snug fit and drawstring waistline pair nicely with a baggy tee or blouse. You can make them shorter or longer, depending on your personal comfort level, and get to relaxing!

SKILL LEVEL
Intermediate

SIZE
XS(S, M, L)
Fits hip circumference: 33(36, 40, 44) in/
 84(91, 102, 112) cm

FINISHED MEASUREMENTS
Hip circumference:
 41½(44½, 48½, 53) in/
 105(113, 123, 135) cm
Total length: 13(14, 15½, 17) in/
 33(35.5, 39, 43) cm

NOTE: These shorts are designed to fit
 loosely and are gathered at the waist
 with a drawstring.

YARN
DK
Filatura di Crosa Zara Chine (100% extra
 fine merino superwash; 137 yds/125 m
 per 50g): 27, oatmeal, 4(4, 5, 5) skeins

NEEDLES
US 8/5 mm circular needle, 24 in/60 cm
 long, *or size needed to obtain gauge*
US 8/5 mm circular needle, 16 in/
 40 cm long

NOTIONS
2 stitch markers (of contrasting colors)
Tapestry needle
Safety pin

GAUGE
20 sts and 30 rows per 4 in/10 cm in
 stockinette stitch, unblocked

INSTRUCTIONS

Waist

Starting at the top of the shorts, and using longer circular needle, CO 164(180, 200, 220) sts.

Join to work in the round, being careful not to twist the work. Place first marker (pm) to indicate beginning of round; this is at the left side of your shorts.

Waistband

Round 1: K82(90, 100, 110), place second marker (pm) to indicate right side, knit to end.

Knit 4 more rounds.

Purl 1 round.

Knit 2 rounds.

Create eyelets for waistband drawstring:

Next round: K39(43, 48, 53), yo, ssk, k2tog, yo, knit to end of round.

Work even until piece measures 3(4, 5, 6) in/7.5(10, 12, 15) cm from beginning.

Shape Hips

Knit 4 rounds.

Increase round: K1, M1L, k to 1 st before marker, M1R, k1, sl marker (sm), k1, M1L, k to 1 st before marker, M1R, k1— 4 sts inc.

Repeat last 5 rounds 10 more times— 208(224, 244, 264) sts.

Work even until piece measures 10(11½, 13, 14) in/25(29, 33, 35.5) cm from cast-on edge.

Divide for Leg Openings and Begin Right Leg

Next round: K54(59, 65, 70) sts and leave them on hold on the cable of the longer circular needle. With shorter circular needle, k100(106, 114, 124) sts, remove marker.

Right leg opening:

Work the 100(106, 114, 124) sts on shorter circular needle for right leg only.

Round 1: Place marker (pm) and join to work in the round.

Next rounds: Work even until leg inseam measures 3(3, 4, 4) in/7.5(7.5, 10, 10) cm, or 1 in/2.5 cm short of desired length.

Next round: Purl.

Next round: Knit.

Repeat last 2 rounds 3 more times.

BO purlwise loosely.

Fasten off. Weave in ends.

Left leg opening:

Turn piece inside out, join yarn, and use the three-needle bind-off (see page 14) to join the first 4(6, 8, 8) sts with the last 4(6, 8, 8) sts that have been held on the longer circular needle. Turn piece right-side out, and using the shorter circular needle, k the rem sts and join them in the round for the left leg— 100(106, 114, 124) sts.

Work as for right leg opening.

Finish Waistband

Turn waistband to the inside of shorts at the purl ridge and pin.

Using the tapestry needle and some of your yarn, sew the cast-on edge of the waistband to the inside of the shorts to create a casing for the drawstring.

Fasten off. Weave in ends.

Drawstring:

Take 3 strands of yarn, each about 8 ft/ 2.4 m long. Tie a knot in one end and braid them. Check the length of your drawstring from time to time. When you have reached the desired length, tie another knot, attach the safety pin to the knot, and feed the drawstring through one eyelet hole at the waist, around the shorts, and out the other eyelet hole.

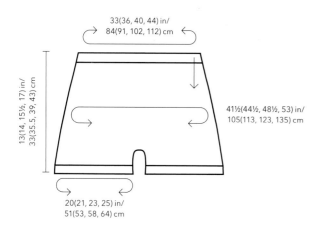

33(36, 40, 44) in/
84(91, 102, 112) cm

13(14, 15½, 17) in/
33(35.5, 39, 43) cm

41½(44½, 48½, 53) in/
105(113, 123, 135) cm

20(21, 23, 25) in/
51(53, 58, 64) cm

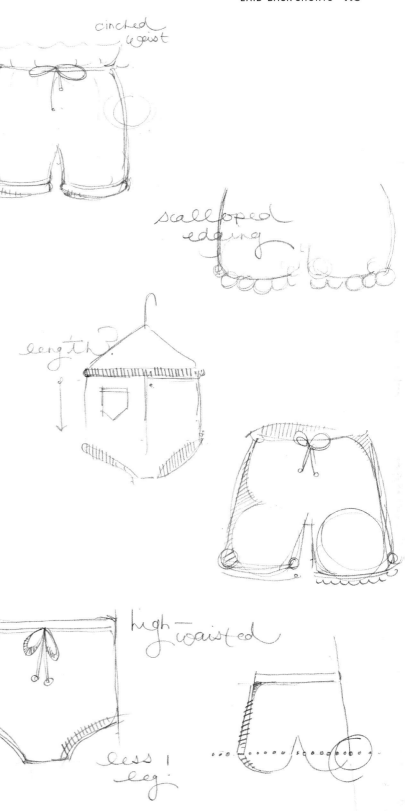

cinched waist

scalloped edging

length

high waisted

less leg.

design inspiration

My goal in designing these shorts was to create a mixture of loungewear and something presentable that could be worn out and about. The laid-back shorts could be paired with comfy wool socks and a baggy tee, while the styled look would be complete with a bright blouse and some bold jewelry. I went with a length that is a bit longer than an average pair of shorts but can easily be adjusted for each individual knitter. The waistband has a drawstring to accommodate a range of different body types and sizes. Overall, these were tough to design because I was concerned about creating a fit that would look good on everyone.

yarn & stitch

Keeping the piece simple and slimming was one of my main goals. I went with a flat stockinette stitch because I didn't want another, more bulky stitch to affect the shaping and overall look of the shorts in an unflattering way.

trial & error

Since we are all shaped so differently, it was important to come up with a design that could be flattering on everyone. Between perfecting the waist and the hips, I had quite a challenge on my hands. I did a lot of measuring, ripping out, and trying on. This is the kind of piece that you have to keep trying on to make sure everything looks okay as you progress. The main areas of effort for me were splitting the two legs and creating a flattering shape.

ZIGZAG SCARF

FELTED EDGING

When designing this neck scarf, I thought about the common criteria for a classic scarf: something that lies flat, looks nice on both sides, and can be paired with many outfits. The rickrack rib stitch was a natural choice because it creates an intricate zigzag pattern that transforms the scarf's surface into an intriguing texture. For a touch of color and flair, I dressed up the edges with colorful felted balls. Get creative by experimenting with size and color of your felt, or just let the scarf stand strongly on its own—it's up to you!

SKILL LEVEL
Beginner

SIZE
One size

FINISHED MEASUREMENTS
Length: 68 in/173 cm
Width: 6 in/15 cm

YARN
Worsted
Cascade Yarns 220 (100% Peruvian Highland wool; 220 yd/201 m per 100 g): 8505 White, 3 skeins

NEEDLES
US 11/8 mm straight needles, *or size needed to obtain gauge*

NOTE: The rickrack rib stitch creates a zigzag pattern that is dense, even on large needles. Plan on using needles 4 to 6 sizes larger than the needle size recommended on the yarn's product information band.

FELTED BALLS
Roving (approximately 3 yd/2.7 m or ⅓ oz/12 g is enough to make 24 felted balls). Roving is a super-bulky-weight length of fleece spun into a long, narrow, fluffy bundle in preparation for spinning. Roving is mainly spun into yarn, but can also be used for projects like, in this case, felting.
Bowl
Hot water
Clear soap (any kind will do)
Towel
Coordinating embroidery thread (about 7 yd/6.4 m)
Embroidery needle

GAUGE
25 sts and 16 rows per 4 in/10 cm in rickrack rib stitch, unblocked

SPECIAL STITCH
Rickrack Rib Stitch
Worked flat over an even number of stitches:
Row 1 (RS): P1, *skip first st, k into back loop of second st (leaving st on left needle), k into front of first st (removing both sts from left needle), P1; repeat from * to end of row.
Row 2 (WS): K1, *p into second st (leaving st on left needle), p into first st (removing both sts from left needle), K1; repeat from * to end of row.
Repeat rows 1 and 2 for rickrack rib st pattern.

INSTRUCTIONS

Body

Starting at one end, CO 40 sts (or any multiple of 3 sts plus 1 st, if you want to vary the width).

Work in the rickrack rib st pattern until piece measures 68 in/173 cm long, or desired length, ending with Row 2.

With RS facing, BO loosely in pattern. Fasten off. Weave in ends.

Felted Balls

1. Divide the roving into 24 pieces, each approximately 4 in/10 cm long.
2. Fill the bowl with the hottest water you can stand to put your hands in.
3. Gently pull apart each piece of roving to loosen the fibers and ready them for felting. Be careful not to pull the fibers completely apart, as this will cause the balls to have cracks in them.
4. Now it's time to begin the felting process. Hold 1 piece of roving in an open palm. Put a very small amount of soap into that same hand. Use your other hand to evenly distribute the soap into the roving with a patting motion. Then gently begin rolling the roving into a ball.
5. Place the piece of roving into the hot water. Pull it out and gently start rolling it again in a circular motion. Don't put a lot of pressure on it at first; let your hands slowly mold it. It takes a minute or two for the ball to take shape and for you to feel like you're making progress, so have patience. If the roving gets too soapy, just dip it in the hot water to rinse it off a bit. The soap mainly helps to move the fiber around in your hands easily, so add soap or rinse it in whatever way feels most workable to you.
6. As the ball cools down, dip it into the hot water again and keep rolling. Continue this process until the ball starts to take shape and get firm.
7. When the ball gets really firm, rinse it in cold water to remove the soap. Remove excess water by rolling the ball on a towel. When you are satisfied with the size and shape of the ball, roll it one last time very tightly in your hands and set it aside to dry.

Attaching felted balls:

1. Cut a piece of the embroidery thread about 10 in/25 cm long and thread it onto the embroidery needle.
2. Push the needle through the center of one felted ball and draw 6 in/15 cm of thread through.
3. Push the needle back into the ball right next to where it came out. Pull the thread all the way through, so the two tails of thread are together. Pull the thread snugly.
4. Use the tails of the thread to attach the felt ball to the two ends of your scarf. Cut the embroidery thread and fasten off. (You may want to plan out the spacing before you begin attaching all the felt balls.) Repeat, for all the felt balls.
5. Thread the embroidery thread ends back onto the embroidery needle and weave them into the edge of the scarf.

design inspiration

Since scarves have such a large surface area to work with, I knew the piece would be perfect for choosing a stitch with a beautiful pattern. Even with an elaborate pattern, I felt like the finished scarf still needed something extra to adorn the edges. Felted balls seemed to offer the terrific pop of color and change of material. I also loved how they dangled and moved when the scarf was being worn.

smaller —or— larger?

yarn & stitch

The rickrack rib stitch that I went with is so graphic and playful, you can't help but want to touch it. This is one of those pieces that will look great in any color you decide to work with—especially if you pick out a good complementary color for the felt balls. When I was deciding on my color palette, I made lots of mini scarf swatches and paired them with different colored felted balls. Felting the balls is easy and fun, so I enjoyed making an array of colors.

trial & error

Figuring out how to attach the felted balls took the most time. I needed a thin material that could be fed through the ball and easily tied onto the scarf. I tried different strings, threads, and yarns, and embroidery thread worked best.

FELTED FLOWERS

FRESH AND COLORFUL

Take your style up a notch by piling on layers of floral accessories. These flowers can be made into decorative brooches or hair clips to provide stunning ways to add some color and texture to your favorite jacket or hairstyle. Cluster them with some fresh flowers in your hair for a true statement (as pictured here). Making these flowers is easy, seamless, and quick, so you can create a bunch of them in no time. This well-rounded project has you knitting, felting, and sewing, so there is lots of opportunity for creativity and personalization.

SKILL LEVEL
Beginner

SIZE
One size

FINISHED MEASUREMENTS
Small flower: 6½ in/16.5 cm square, before felting
Large flower: 9 in/23 cm square, before felting
Leaf: 2¼ by 3¼ in/5.5 by 8 cm, before felting

YARN
Worsted
Cascade Yarns 220 (100% Peruvian Highland wool; 220 yd/183 m per 100 g): 9421 Blue Hawaii, 2433 Pacific, 7804 Shrimp, and 7802 Cerise

For 1 small flower: approximately 40 yd/ 36.5 m
For 1 large flower: approximately 75 yd/ 68.5 m
For 1 leaf: approximately 4 yd/3.7 m
NOTE: If you are substituting yarns, be sure to use a pure wool yarn that isn't "superwash" so that the piece will felt.

NEEDLES
US 11/8 mm straight needles, *or size needed to obtain gauge*

NOTIONS
Tapestry needle

FELTING
Hot water
Pot or kettle to boil water
Bowl
Cold water
Clear soap (any kind will do)

Putting Felted Pieces Together
Scrap paper
Pencil
Scissors
Sewing needle
Coordinating thread (to match yarn colors)
Brooch pin back (½ in/12 mm long) (optional)
Barrette-style hair clip (1 in/2.5 cm long) (optional)

GAUGE
16 sts and 30 rows per 4 in/10 cm in garter stitch, unblocked
NOTE: Matching gauge is not crucial in this project.

INSTRUCTIONS

Small Flower

CO 25 sts.
Knit all rows (garter st) until piece
    measures 6½ in/16.5 cm.
BO.
Fasten off. Weave in ends with the
    tapestry needle.

Large Flower

CO 35 sts.
Knit all rows (garter st) until piece
    measures 9 in/23 cm.
BO.
Fasten off. Weave in ends.

Leaf

CO 3 sts.
Row 1: K1, kfb, k1—4 sts.
Rows 2, 4, 6, 8, and 10: Purl.
Row 3: K1, kfb, kfb, k1—6 sts.
Row 5: K1, kfb, k2, kfb, k1—8 sts.
Row 7: K1, kfb, k4, kfb, k1—10 sts.
Row 9: K1, k2tog, k to last 3 sts, ssk, k1—
    8 sts.
Repeat rows 9 and 10 two more times—
    4 sts rem.
BO.
Fasten off. Weave in ends.

Felting the pieces:

1. Prepare the hot and cold water baths.
   I usually boil the water on the stove to
   make it really hot and then let it sit for
   a bit so I don't burn myself. The hotter
   the better, but be careful!

2. Fully submerge your knitted piece in
   the hot water. Stir it around for about
   10 minutes to get the fibers agitated,
   open, and ready for felting.

3. Remove from hot water, wring out,
   and put into cold water. The process
   of going from hot to cold shocks the
   fibers and tangles them together
   permanently. Remove from the cold
   water, and squeeze out the water.

4. Put the piece back into hot water. Begin
   to scrub your piece within your hands,
   using a bit of the soap to provide the
   perfect amount of friction. Do a combination of rubbing, rolling, and scrub-
   bing. The process is slow at first but
   keep at it and be patient! One thing to
   be careful of is losing the shape of your
   knitted piece as you felt it. It's very easy
   for it to take on a life of its own as you
   rub it every which way. Keep your eye
   on the shape throughout the process
   and smooth it out if it starts to morph.

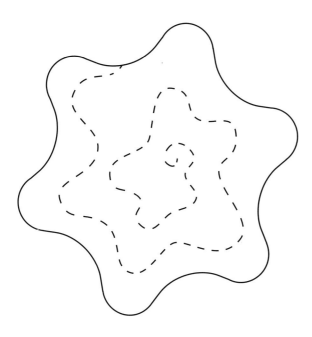

Flower Template
Enlarge 200% for large flower.

5. After a few minutes, put it back in the cold water and squeeze out the water.

6. Continue steps 4 and 5 until your piece is fully felted: it will take on a solid texture in which you can no longer see stitches.

Shaping flower with leaf:

At this point, you should have a felted leaf and a felted square (small or large depending on which size you're making).

1. Enlarge the template (if necessary), cut out, and place it over your felted square. Pin in place.

2. Cut out the flower shape.

3. Starting at any point on the shape, cut in a spiral toward the center, following the outline of the shape. Once you near the center, finish the spiral off with a small circle that will act as the bottom of your flower. (One joy of working with felted wool is that cut edges don't ravel, so you won't have to finish the edges of the spiral.)

4. Thread the sewing needle with a color that coordinates with the flower you're making.

5. Take the outside end of the spiral and start rolling it tightly until you reach the end on the inside. As you do this, you will see the flower come to life as a rosette. The small circle you made in the center will act as a platform for you to attach a brooch pin or a hair clip, if using.

6. Sew the flower together, starting at the bottom. Work around until all the petals are secure. You can check this by gently pulling on different layers.

7. To attach the leaf, thread the sewing needle with a coordinating color. Decide where you would like the leaf to sit on your flower, leaving enough room to attach the pin back or hair clip. Sew the leaf securely in place.

8. To attach the pin back or hair clip, if desired, use the sewing needle and coordinating thread to sew the hardware onto the flat platform at the bottom of the flower.

design inspiration

I designed these flowers to be little color-ful details that you could quickly add on to enhance your look. I started out by researching different types and shapes of flowers. Did I want roses, daisies, tons of petals or only a few? I also asked myself how I would be assembling these and what limitations that might create. Would I be sewing them together, felting them with roving and a felting needle, or would some kind of glue work? I also wondered how small I could go without making them too difficult to assemble.

yarn & stitch

Since I would be felting all of the knitted pieces, I had to use 100 percent wool. Colors are important to me, so I searched for a brand of wool that had a wide range of hues and shades that would be good choices for floral designs. I have loads of experience with Cascade 220 and their palette, which is perfect for these flowers.

trial & error

I started out making individual petals and assembling them into one flower, but I had trouble making these flowers look clean, consistent, and finished. My end results always came out messy and looked like they would fall apart at any minute. So I got creative. I felted a square, and then came up with a way to cut out one shape that could be sewn into a flower. It's seamless, easy, and durable.

BALLOON SWEATER

SHAPELY SLEEVES

I like my sweaters extra big, almost like I'm wearing my boyfriend's clothes that are five sizes too large for me! When designing this sweater, I wanted something that would be fitted and flattering in some areas, while baggy and comfortable in others. With its formfitting body, flared sleeves, and seed stitch pattern, this piece is all about the chunky texture and interesting proportions.

SKILL LEVEL
Intermediate

SIZE
XS(S, M, L)
Fits bust circumference up to:
  32(36, 40, 44) in/81(91, 102, 112) cm

FINISHED MEASUREMENTS
Bust circumference: 36(40, 44, 49 in/
  91(102, 112, 124.5) cm
Length: 21½(22½, 23½, 24) in/
  54(57, 60, 61) cm

YARN
Bulky
Rowan Sweet Harmony by Amy Butler
  (100% merino wool; 87 yd/80 m per
  100 g): 132 Frost, 8(9, 9, 10) skeins

NEEDLES
US 10.5/6.5 mm circular needle, 24 in/
  60 cm long, *or size needed to
  obtain gauge*
US 10.5/6.5 mm circular, 16 in/
  40 cm long

NOTIONS
Stitch markers (of contrasting colors)
Stitch holder or scrap yarn (optional)
Tapestry needle

GAUGE
13 sts and 26 rows per 4 in/10 cm in
  seed stitch, unblocked

SPECIAL STITCH
Seed Stitch
Worked in the round over an even
  number of stitches:
Round 1: *K1, p1; repeat from * to end.
Round 2: *P1, k1; repeat from * to end.
Repeat Rounds 1 and 2 for seed stitch
  pattern.

Worked flat over an odd number
  of stitches:
All rows: *K1, p1; repeat from * to last
  st, k1.

INSTRUCTIONS

This sweater is worked wholly in seed stitch pattern. Starting at the bottom edge, using the longer circular needle, CO 118(130, 142, 158).

Join to work in the round, being careful not to twist the work. Place marker (pm) to indicate beginning of round (this will be at your left-side seam).

Work in seed st pattern (in the round) until piece measures 14(14½, 15, 15) in/ 35.5(37, 38, 38) cm from cast-on edge.

Front

Work across 59(65, 71, 79) sts in pattern. Turn.

You are now working on the front stitches only. The stitches for the back can be held on the cable of your circular needle or on a stitch holder or a piece of scrap yarn. You will still be using a circular needle, but you will be working flat, turning at the end of each row.

Next row (WS): Sl1 st purlwise with yarn in front, and continue in seed st to the end of row.

Next row (RS): Sl1 st purlwise with yarn in back, and continue in seed st to the end of row.

Repeat the last two rows until piece measures 5½(6, 6½, 7) in/14(15, 16.5, 18) cm from where you divided front from back, ending with a WS row.

Neck shaping:

Work across 20(23, 25, 29) sts, BO center 19(19, 21, 21) sts, work to end of row. You will now be working each shoulder separately.

Right shoulder:

Next row (WS): Sl1, work to end in seed st (working flat).

Next row (RS): Sl1, k3tog, work to end.

Repeat last 2 rows 2 more times—14(17, 19, 23) sts.

Work until armhole measures 7½(8, 8½, 9) in/19(20, 21.5, 23) cm.

Cut yarn.

Place stitches on a holder or scrap yarn and set aside.

Left shoulder:

Working again on the longer circular needle, join yarn at the neck edge.

Next row (WS): Sl1, work even in seed stitch (working flat).

Next row (RS): Sl1, work to last 4 sts, k3tog, p1.

Repeat last 2 rows twice more—14(17, 19, 23) sts.

Work even until armhole measures 7½(8, 8½, 9) in/19(20, 21.5, 23) cm.

Cut yarn.

Place sts on a stitch holder or scrap yarn and set aside.

Back

Working on the longer circular needle, join yarn with RS facing.

Work even in seed st on these 59(65, 71, 79) sts until armhole measures 6½(7, 7½, 8) in/16.5(18, 19, 20) cm, ending with a WS row.

Neck shaping:

Work across 18(21, 23, 27) sts, BO center 23(23, 25, 25) sts, work to end of row. You will now be working each shoulder separately.

Right shoulder:

Next row (WS): Sl1, work in seed st (working flat) to end.

Next row (RS): Sl1, k3tog, work to end.

Repeat last 2 rows 1 more time— 14(17, 19, 23) sts.

Work even until armhole measures 7½(8, 8½, 9) in/19(20, 21.5, 23) cm.

Join front and back right shoulder with three-needle bind-off (see page 14).

Cut yarn.

Left shoulder:

Working with longer circular needle, join yarn at neck edge.

Next row (WS): Sl1, work in seed stitch (working flat) to end of row.

Next row (RS): Sl1, work to last 4 sts, k3tog, p1.

Repeat last 2 rows 1 more time—14(17, 19, 23) sts.

Work even until armhole measures 7½(8, 8½, 9) in/19(20, 21.5, 23) cm.

Join front and back right shoulder edges with three-needle bind-off.

Cut yarn.

Sleeves (work both the same)

Working with the shorter circular needle, starting at the underarm, pick up and knit 48(52, 56, 60) sts around the armhole, place a marker, and join to work in the round, being careful not to twist the work.

Work in seed st (in the round) until piece measures 11(11, 11½, 11½) in/28(28, 29, 29) cm from underarm, ready to start the round with a knit stitch.

Shape balloon sleeve:

Next round: [Work 8 sts in seed st, kfb twice] 4(5, 5, 6) times, work to end of round—56(62, 66, 72) sts.

Work 7(7, 9, 9) rounds even.

Next round: [Work 10 sts in seed st, kfb twice] 4(5, 5, 6) times, work to the end of round—64(72, 76, 84) sts.

Knit rounds even until piece measures 20(20½, 20½, 21) in/50.5(52, 52, 53) cm from underarm, ending with a round that starts with a purl st.

Last round: *k3tog, p3tog; repeat from * to last 4(0, 4, 0) sts, k3tog, p1.

BO loosely.

Cut yarn.

FINISHING

Fasten off. Weave in ends with the tapestry needle.

Lightly block.

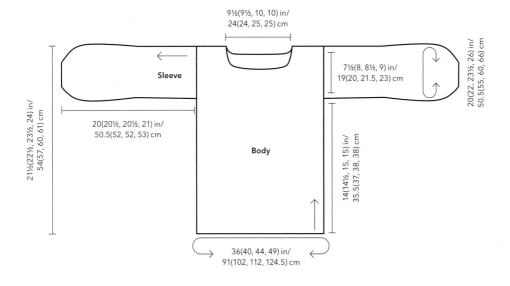

design inspiration

When I started brainstorming for this project, I asked myself: How could I make the familiar sweater into something completely fresh and original? Since I like to wear some of my clothes baggier, when I was sketching, I played around with the idea of an oversize fit. Making the body of the sweater baggy resulted in an unflattering look, so I worked on the shoulders and arms. By keeping the neck and shoulders fitted and the arms and wrists ballooned, I successfully achieved the ideal shape.

yarn & stitch

I combined the seed stitch with a chain-constructed yarn to create a textured and chunky look. The finished fabric draws you in and makes you want to feel it, and the super-bulky yarn makes the finished piece as thick and substantial as I wanted.

trial & error

I had to knit the sleeves a few times before I got them exactly right. The first time, I overshot and made them massively wide. So I slimmed down the width of the ballooned areas. These sleeves were done separately, in the round, so it was just a matter of increasing and decreasing stitches to get the proper shape.

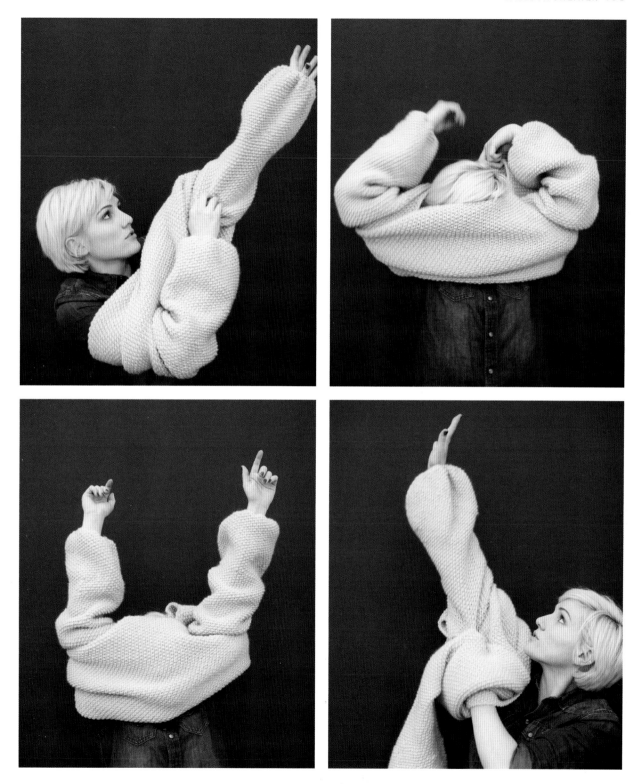

RESOURCES

BOOKS AND MAGAZINES

400 Knitting Stitches: A Complete Dictionary of Essential Stitch Patterns, **by Crown Publishing Group**
A dictionary of stitches for any knitting style or skill level.

Cast On, Bind Off: 54 Step-by-Step Methods, **by Leslie Ann Bestor**
You'll never run out of ideas for the beginning and ending for a project with this book in hand.

Designing Knitwear, **by Deborah Newton**
Learn everything there is to know about knitwear design from a skilled veteran.

The Fleece & Fiber Sourcebook: More Than 200 Fibers, from Animal to Spun Yarn, **by Carol Ekarius and Deborah Robson**
A comprehensive, informative encyclopedia of animal fibers.

KnitKnit: Profiles and Projects from Knitting's New Wave, **by Sabrina Gschwandtner**
An inspiring look into the lives of twenty-seven talented fine art knitters.

The Knitting Book, **by Frederica Patmore and Vicki Haffenden**
From the basics to more advanced techniques, this book has everything knitters need to create beautiful items for their homes and wardrobes.

Vogue Knitting: The Ultimate Knitting Book, **by Vogue Magazine Knitting Editors**
A comprehensive guide by many of the leading experts in knitwear design.

ONLINE INSPIRATION

Allforeveryone.com
Annie Larson creates intricate pattern work and color combinations.

Knitdreams.tumblr.com
A knitting blog with a gorgeous collection of images, colors, and textures.

Knittingdaily.com
An online community with an endless amount of helpful and inspiring resources.

Onesheepishgirl.blogspot.com
Meredith Crawford, a Dallas-based blogger, shares her adventures in knitting and what inspires her.

Pinterest.com
A great resource for gathering visual inspiration.

Ravelry.com
A social media site that is great for sharing and finding new ideas, projects, yarns, and tools.

Vogueknitting.com
The ultimate website and publication for trends and fashionable designs.

Woolandthegang.com
A DIY fashion brand that is paving the way in stylish and youthful knitwear.

FASHION AND STREET STYLE

Thecoveteur.com
Take a look inside the homes and closets of today's tastemakers and icons.

Garancedore.fr/en
A major fashion enthusiast and illustrator who blogs about her inspiring and beautiful surroundings.

Thelocals.dk
A refined compilation of street-style portraiture.

Thesartorialist.com
Fashion photographer Scott Schuman gives us a look into the world of street fashion and its relationship to daily life.

INDEX

ACKNOWL-EDGMENTS

I'd like to thank the people who supported, helped, and guided me as I wrote this book: My editor, Lisa Tauber, who believed in me enough to give me this amazing opportunity. Kristi Porter and Ellen Wheat, for all of your editing expertise. Krista Knutson, who was by my side throughout the entire process: this book wouldn't have been possible without you. Cora Innes, who was there with a second pair of hands when I couldn't juggle it all. Max Wanger, who captured images of all of my hard work in such a unique and beautiful way; the end result is perfect in my eyes because of your skill and patience. Ali Brislin, for her styling genius and production assistance. Kelly Shew, for her talented skills in hair and makeup. Kate Miss, Melanie Ayer, Jen Coleman, and Beth Poploski for modeling the knitted pieces better than I have ever seen! My family and close friends, who have always been fully supportive of my creative walk. And thank you Yeah!Rentals, The Impossible Project, BC Footwear, Katie Rodgers, Young Frankk, Kate Miss Jewelry, Adored Vintage, Individual Medley, and Madewell, for your generosity toward making the photographs in this book shine.